als ∘ ∘Cereals∘

T0313651

HAVE YOU EVER THOUGHT
JUST WHAT
CANNED FOODS MEAN TO YOU

WRAPPING IT UP

50 years of British packaging design
1920–1970

Ruth Artmonsky & Stella Harpley

While more and more artists and designers have been applying themselves constructivley to the problems of the poster and the press advertisment, packet design remains almost a virgin field. The packet represents, in a way, the last link in the chain of propoganda done on behalf of the product it contains. The fact that, at the present moment, it is the weakest link is not only bad art but bad salesmanship.

Ashley Havinden, 1934

Published by Artmonsky Arts
Flat 1, 27 Henrietta Street
London WC2E 8NA
Telephone: 020 7240 8774
Email: artmonskyruth@gmail.com

ISBN 978-0-9935878-8-7

The cover design has been adapted from Leonard Beaumont's
Fare for All Sainsbury's poster. End papers from Bowater Papers

The illustration opposite the title page is from a *Metal Box*
booklet produced 1930s

The illustration on the previous page is from *Sales
Appeal & Packaging Technology*, 1962. The Ashley
Havinden Quote is from, *Shelf Appeal*, July 1934

Opposite: Illustration from *Package & Print*, 1947

My thanks to Stella for all the help in researching and collecting
ephemera and editing; to Eduardo Sant Anna for the 'to-ing and
fro-ing' he has had to do and to Brian Webb and Flora Anderson
for their delightful design and enthusiam which have contributed
so considerably to the book.

Designed by Webb & Webb Design Limited
Printed in England by Northend Creative Print Solutions

CONTENTS

INTRODUCTION

It may seem perverse to write a book about packaging as both a necessity and a delight, when our oceans, beaches and countryside are being desecrated by it.

Packaging and its design is a complex matter involving lots of people, much knowledge, many skills, and, obviously, the vested interests of both manufacturers and consumers, all needing careful consideration before one is swept away by heated emotions, often justified but often over-simplified, urging one to get rid of as much of it as possible. My own totally separate axe to grind, which I have done in many of my previous books, has been about the under-valuation of 'commercial' artists, who have produced, at times, iconic images within the constraints of a brief, a budget and a deadline, compared to the overvaluation of the so-called 'fine' artists, motivated nowadays largely by their own egos, and sometimes with an eye on what the agents and galleries may be prepared to hype, and the gullible prepared to pay.

Previously I have largely concerned myself with graphic artists working in advertising and publicity, but now my focus has shifted to those who have applied themselves to packaging design, either on a surface level or with basic package construction. Inadvertently I have chosen a subject that is highly political but I would ask the reader to take another look at packaging before disposing of it. The purpose of the book is to explain some of the complexities of package design and for the reader to admire the ingenuity and artistry of the package designer. If, incidentally, it helps readers to make better informed and balanced decisions on where they stand on the packaging issues, so much the better.

Opposite: The River Thames at Limehouse

THE DEVLOPMENT OF PACKAGING

'Among the many branches of commercial art one of the most fascinating, perhaps, is the developing of Wrappings and Packings. It is a field which is, at present, practically untouched and yet is very great and varied.' **Commercial Art 1924**

Packaging, presumably, might be traced back to pre-history, when primitive man turned to whatever was at hand – a leaf, a gourd, tree bark or animals' innards – to wrap something he valued and wanted to keep or carry from one place to another. Much has been made of examples such as Egyptian pots for eye-shadow and Greek and Roman amphora and the likes, but Jankowski's *Shelf Life* has 'modern' packaging, and one might even say branding, dating to around 1550, when a German paper maker wrapped bundles of his stock with paper –

'with a printed design…a spirited woodcut of a horse, his name, and his shop's location'

Opposite: Packaging becomes crucial with the coming of supermarkets
Above: Automatic packaging, an early packaging machine

There are tales of early book publishers who, when unbound books were not selling well, passed the pages on to apothecaries and grocers as wrapping paper. Although there was some formal packaging for such products as quack medicines, tobacco, tea, pins and playing cards by the 18th century, for many goods, for many well into the 20th century, it was a matter of their being delivered in bulk to a retailer. It would then be the retailer's job to cut or scoop quantities to be weighed and carefully wrapped to the requirements of the customer. Even in the 1940s grocery assistants, in such chains as Lipton's and Home & Colonial, would meticulously cut slices of cheese or butter from an anonymous block whilst the customer waited patiently, meanwhile discussing some snippet of neighbourhood news.

It was only in the 19th century that manufacturers began to appreciate, to any extent, that packaging could serve beyond

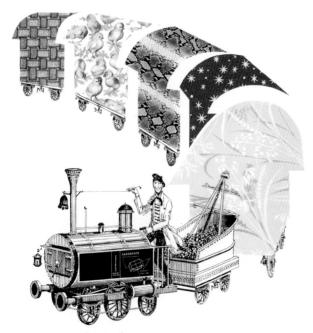

You can rest assured that a packaging or box paper from Sanderson does just what you want it to do. Patterned or plain, bright shades or light shades, there's a whole lively world to choose from—a paper for every product, more colours than a paint box ever dreamed of. Wrap with distinction—sell with Sanderson.

SANDERSON packaging and display papers
BERNERS STREET, LONDON, W.1.

BIRDS AND BEASTS —
BOTTLED BY UNITED GLASS

The Laughing Jackglass

PLUMAGE: Multi-coloured (flint, pale, green, amber, blue, opal).
DIET: Food and drink and thousands of other good things.
HABITAT: United Glass, the place to go for the best glass packaging service.

- The finest in modern glass package design and research.
- Containers and closures made together to suit each other perfectly.
- Expert help and advice on any glass packaging problem.
- The right type of container for every kind of product.

Glass makes the finest containers of all — and United Glass makes them by the million. Let us know how we can help you.

UNITED GLASS

UNITED GLASS LTD., LEICESTER HOUSE, LEICESTER SQUARE, LONDON, W.C.2.
TELEPHONE : GERRARD 8611. TELEGRAMS : GLASPAK, LESQUARE, LONDON.

Advertisments from *Sales Appeal & Packaging Technology*, 1961

Advertisments from *Sales Appeal*, 1952 and *Design for Industry*, 1959

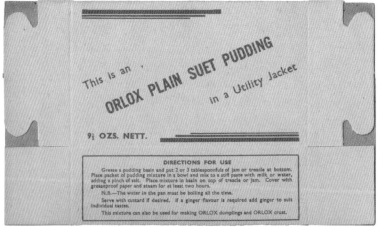

Orlox packaging prior to World War II and with a war-time utility pack

its function of protecting a product to actually enhancing the goodwill of the company producing the product, and to possibly increasing sales; and this came about with the growth of branding. For some time manufacturers of such commodities as cloth and drink had branded bales and casks with simple devices to show ownership; and from such primitive marks would morph elaborate packaging and labelling often bearing not only the mark of the manufacturer but his name and even his image and that of his factory, along with wordy hypes of the exceptional qualities of the product so wrapped. The tobacco manufacturer, W.D. & H.O. Wills began such branding as early as the 1840s, and, by the turn of the century, branding had become so commonplace, that the government found it necessary to bring in a series of Trademark Acts to curb counterfeiting and plagiarism.

This more sophisticated branding necessitated package design and frequently this fell into the lap of printers who began to expand their services, some even going into package production as well as printing, as, for example, when Huntley, Bourne & Stevens took out a patent for printing on tin and became the largest firm of tin box makers in Victorian times, helped, no doubt, by Huntley's family connection with Huntley & Palmer, the Reading biscuit makers. By the 1890s a new kind of firm had emerged, at least when it came to the use of tin in packaging, one which designed, manufactured and printed for brands, soon to be used by such competing biscuit makers as Carr's and Peek Frean, along with Will's and some pharmaceutical companies, such as Allen & Hanburys.

By the 1920s there were a myriad of firms, small and large, general and specialised, providing packaging for manufacturers as Barclay & Fry, Metal Box, United Glass, and British Aluminium, along with some product manufacturers who decided it was worthwhile to have their own packaging construction departments.

Although canning (sealed tins compared to a tin container with a lid) was known about in the early 19th century, it took a series of wars, with the need to feed hordes of troops on the move, to develop the idea. Early essays came from Europe, but it was the Americans who fully mechanised canning for mass civilian markets. Metal Box, by a series of astute commercial moves, became one of the largest suppliers in Britain, but many product producers, including Smedleys. Batchelors, Cross & Blackwell and Heinz, installed their own canning plants.

With the growth of the packaging industry on the back of branding came another crucial factor in its development – mechanisation. Initially much package construction and package filling was done by hand, a good deal of the latter by women. But, bit by bit, machinery was introduced for the different parts of the packaging process, Horniman's Tea having its first packaging machine as early as the 1830s, and machines for making and cutting cardboard for packaging were in use by the 1880s. Rose Brothers got its first patent in 1881 when William Rose, totally untutored, took his ideas for packaging to Will's of Bristol, and from such beginnings grew one of the major British company's producing packaging machinery. Initially the machines for each aspect would stand alone, the product being produced transported from one to another by hand; gradually the whole operation

Combined Operation

Rose and Forgrove together supply packaging
machines to the world's leading names in frozen foods.

ROSE BROTHERS (Gainsborough) LTD Albion Works Gainsborough · Gainsborough 2231
THE FORGROVE MACHINERY CO LTD Dewsbury Road Leeds 11. Tel: Leeds 75222

Members of the Baker Perkins Group
RF 7A

Advertisment for Rose Brothers, pioneers of packaging machinery, 1962

became automated. By the 1920s and 30s there were machines for weighing, filling, capping or sealing, bottle washing, packing, printing, strapping, counting, embossing, glueing, labelling, wrapping, tying, stitching – practically everything that was needed.

And along with mechanization was the development of an enormous range of new materials suitable for packaging. By 1924 there were, for example, 500 fibres alone from which paper could be made, each with its own utilitarian qualities. The Penrose Annual for 1933 gave some idea of the materials used in packaging at the time, including paper products, when telling of the challenges they gave to the printer –

'He must print on bags, on boxes, on cartons,
on labels, on parchments, on papers dry-waxed,
self-sealing waxed, moisture-proofed waxed,
metallic coated, plated, tissue, manila, transparent
cellulose, pyroxene coated, flint, velour,
friction glazed, mica, multi-colour, wood grain;
of foils of several hundred different grades;
on cardboard of various weights; on cork, on cloth.'

The advantages and disadvantages of using one material rather than another had to be weighed against such criteria as cost, protection of contents, durability, pliability and so on; each material had its pluses and minuses – customers could see the product itself through glass or cellophane, tin was light in weight, aluminium was non-toxic and did not transmit light, whilst

16

ceramics had the attraction that once the contents had been used up the container could serve as a dish or a vase, or such like.

A traumatic shift in available materials for packaging designers was the arrival of plastics. Generally considered a 20th century development, in fact one, Alexander Parkes of Birmingham, had launched his Parkesine in the 1850s – 'hard as horn, but as flexible as leather, capable of being cast or stamped, painted, dyed or carved'. Cellophane, one of the earliest plastics to be used widely for packaging, was on the market in Britain before WWI, although not used extensively until the 1930s. By 1936 the annual *Packaging Omnibus* felt confident enough to declare that 'plastics are now far beyond the novelty stage'.

It was in the post-WWII years that the range of plastics available for packaging expanded exponentially – to cellophane and cellulose were added polystyrene, polythene, polyvinyl chloride, nylon, polypropylene, PVC, and many more. By the early 1960s the British Standards Institute felt compelled to publish lists of common names and abbreviations for the plastics pouring, as it were, on to the market, and Metal Box was complaining 'keeping up with the Joneses is becoming something of a nightmare in the plastics packing

Metal Box, a major supplier of aerosol containers, *Sales Appeal*, 1961

industry.' And with the arrival of aerosols, vacuum packs, and the like, the combinations and permutations open to the package designer were countless.

But perhaps the most crucial of all factors affecting packaging development was the arrival of self-service for shopping, and the coming of supermarkets. As with so many aspects of the retail industry the Americans had taken a lead introducing a form of self-service not long after WWI, whilst Britain only really got enthusiastic about the idea after WWII. Self-service, obviously, could not have happened without branding, for the goods had to 'shout out' for themselves on the shelves. Procter & Gamble referred to the required impact as 'the first moment of truth', stressing that first impressions were crucial. With self-service customers could shop at what speed they liked and could find most of their staple needs under one roof. The 1950s saw most of the grocery chains open self-service supermarkets – Express Dairies, Sainsbury's, Tesco's.

Branding, mechanisation, developments in the material sciences and self-service, all contributed to moving packaging and packaging design from a Cinderella position to centre stage.

PACKAGING DESIGN

PROTECTION

Writers on the history of packaging have became increasingly interested in its service as a medium for advertising, and have tended to put its protective function to the background as an altogether less interesting and certainly less glamorous aspect, as with The Design Council's publication *Packaging Design,* 1991, almost entirely focused on the marketing potential of a wrapping. But any product has to pass from the manufacturer to the wholesaler and/or retailer and on to the consumer in a pristine state and maintain it as long as is necessary. In such a journey, by road, rail, sea or air, its packaging is exposed to a series of possible 'dangers', and it is to these that designers of packaging must initially address themselves.

A package may be knocked, dropped, scratched, vibrated, and buffeted; may be permeated both biologically and climatically – by fungi, mould, bacteria, insects, vermin, light, heat, cold and moisture. And along with these 'dangers' from the outside, leakage or spillage of contents from the inside must be prevented.

Further the designer needs to consider how the package will be used in the shop and in the home – opened, resealed and stored; if the product is dangerous, is it sufficiently protected from prying little hands, and so on. The designer Hulme-Chadwick humorously addressed a Cake and Biscuit Alliance audience in 1964 on the matter –

> *'the difficulty met by the consumer who first looks in vain for a suitable opening, then immerses himself in several layers, ranging through cellophane and grease-proof paper to corrugated card, usually managing at the end to break several biscuits or to stick his finger through perfect icing.'*

And, as has been already noted, it was the breakability of biscuits that led to one of the early essays into packaging when the baker Thomas Huntley, swamped by demands from coaching

Opposite: Traditional packaging in the age of modernism, 1938

passengers, called in his brother, a tinsmith, to start on the design of the biscuit tins that are now collectors' items.

SHAPE

Objects to be wrapped come in all shapes and sizes and the package designer has to accommodate this. From golf and tennis balls to cutlery and scent bottles and eggs, all have their challenge for the designer who has a range of three-dimensional possibilities from which to choose for a solution – pyramids, spheres, cones, cylinders, and the more common cubes and rectangular prisms (boxes); but the more courageous could experiment with totally irregular shapes as one tightly silhouetting the product.

Cosmetics gift packaging by Willy de Majo, 1959

for display, and stacking that is economical of space in the average home kitchen. This has led most packaging designers to resort to the simple cube or box shape with some kind of internal structure to hold the product tightly as with egg boxes, bottle carrying packs or packets for light bulbs. Only the more risk-taking designer would argue for a 'novelty' shape as de Majo with his pyramid for perfume or Derek Mills with his triangular 'Tetra Pack' for Express Dairy Milk.

A further aspect of shape – size – is also key when it comes to stacking for economy of space. Sometimes designers were tempted, or actually encouraged, to provide a much larger pack than was necessary so that the product should not look insignificant when compared to its competitors. And height has continued to be a consideration with such products as breakfast cereals and olive oils when it comes to fitting into the standard kitchen cupboard shelving.

The key criterion when it comes to shape is 'stacking' – for moving products from factory to warehouse to retailer to home – stacking that is secure for protection, stacking that is attractive

Charlton in his *The Art of Packaging* played it safe when it

came to shape concluding –

> *'Unless there is a substantial reason for departure from the general type, it is safer to stick to the package of established standards.'*

COLOUR

Although the colour of a pack and its decoration is frequently mentioned by writers on packaging and is considered key as to why someone would notice one pack rather than another, for the period covered by this book which colour to use, in which way, in what circumstances, seems to have been more a matter of folklore and personal prejudice than supported by experimental evidence. It is said that the colours for Campbell's soup can labels came from a director struck by the colours worn by his local football team.

So, in folklore, blue has tended to imply spirituality (the sky, the Virgin Mary's dress); brown an earthy warmth (brown eggs, little brown jug); red – excitement and strength (red-blooded, red-letter day); yellow – cheerfulness (sunlight); green – fertility (spring growth); black – sophistication (little black dress); white – innocence (angels), and so on. Yet for each colour there is also, in folklore, an opposite – black – death, blue – depression, red – danger, etc. A good deal of what is written about colour has little objective basis and is often fatuous. Mona Doyle, in her book, says that cereal packets should be in light bright colours as their contents are eaten in morning light; and that gourmet dinners should be in deep rich colours to set a mood of elegance and luxury. Even Charlton in his textbook suggests –

> *'packages which go into the home wisely refrain from too garish and crude a colour treatment, as they may be offensive to women.'*

Some 'scientific' research into reactions to colour was going on during this period, so that it was established that seeing red causes the body to pump adrenalin, making the heart beat faster, and infants would look at red in preference to any other colour; along with such niceties that women preferred a blue-based red and men favoured a yellow-based one. But much of this would be too subtle for manufacturers and certainly doesn't seem to have reached public circulation.

Triangular TetraPak designed by Derek Mills for Express Dairy, 1959

Soap powder in strong colours

For the packaging designer the considerations are that the colour should distinguish the product and that the physical qualities of the colour are suitable for its use – does it look as attractive in artificial light on a shop shelf as in daylight; will the ink be likely to fade; how easy is it to print on the surface chosen; what are its reflective qualities; how will it combine with the typography to be used, and so on.

Colour has certainly come to the aid of designers when dealing with the packaging for families of products where it is essential to maintain a brand image yet to distinguish the subgroups. Hans Schleger, designing packaging for Mac Fisheries, chose blue for fish, green for vegetables, red for fruit, pink for shellfish and brown for fish paste. Milner Gray wrote of his choice of colour when designing packaging for Ilford's –

'white and blue were selected as the new house colours, white being chosen for its distinctiveness. Having chosen white as the background colour it was then possible to rationalize the designs. Black on white with black symbols was to be the design for Ilford black-and-white films; paper and chemicals supplemented by product colour codes.'

Consumers became loyal to a brand colour. It was reported that when Kodak briefly changed to blue packaging in 1914, sales dropped, but its fortunes were restored when it returned to an orangey yellow against which black type stood out strongly.

Reviewing the whole use of colour in packaging the academics, Hope and Welch, concluded that it was the simple primaries that worked best and that 'subtlety goes unnoticed'. Certainly, at that time, there seems to have been insufficient research evidence of any hard wiring between specific colours and specific emotions that many marketing people and designers seem to have been so sure about.

TYPOGRAPHY

Norbert Dutton, in praise of type, wrote 'a line of lettering can give as much purely aesthetic pleasure as a piece of music or poetry'; nevertheless when it came to the use of type on packaging he was severely practical, as when he advised that the less that was written on the front of any pack 'the more forcefully it speaks'.

Designers have relative luxury when given a carton's surfaces to play with – top, bottom, front, back and sides – on which to layout the required information, when compared to the challenge of getting the message on to a label. The words to be used are usually determined by the company's marketing department or its advertising agent, along with those the government sees as essential; it is for the designer to suggest what should go where, in what size, typeface and colour, and in what relation to any images being used. For example, for any carton the following are usually included –

Above and opposite: from *Women's Realm*, 1958

The product name

The company name

The contents/ingredients

Directions for use

Net weight/size of contents (*without wrapper*)

Legally required info.

Promotional message

Much early packaging also included the price, (particularly when there was a price war going on), and would often try and cram as much of the information as possible on to the front of a package. Over time it became more customary to have minimal wording on the front, as Dutton had advised, and relegate much of the information to the other surfaces.

Obviously the main criterion for lettering on packaging is that it should not only be visible but legible, otherwise it would fall at the first fence. But, as with total packaging design, type needs also to contribute to attracting the customer to buy, and, having bought once to buy again. Most designers have made use of what typeface was available at the time, but some created their own, as when Ashley Havinden rebranded for Liberty's in the late 40s and the 50s.

Choosing an appropriate typeface is no easy matter for there are literally hundreds of typefaces available, the number increasing astronomically from the 1930s onwards. Alec Davis was more than somewhat cynical when he wrote in his *Type in Advertising* –

> *'No company chairman has yet announced to his shareholders that their increased dividend was earned by using Corvinus Skyline instead of Cooper Black…'*

To the average viewer the differences between typefaces might well not even be noticed, but the sensitive designer could agonise interminably as to size and curves of serif, or thickness of stroke. Until the 1930s most typefaces had been created for books, magazines and newsprint and not for advertising and packaging, and many did not transfer well. One might search in vain through journals devoted to typography for any mention of its use for commercial purposes. Howard Milton in his *Packaging Design* for the Design Council echoes Davis' cynicism –

> *'…the standard use of typographic styles adds little to the business of creating a unique or memorable brand.'*

but admitted that the colouring used for lettering could make an impact. Immediately the red of the Kellogg's Cornflakes logo

The evolution of a label, left and middle are initial designs by Edward Bawden. On the right the final design using Bawden's illustration but typography by the brewer's advertising agency, 1950s

ABCDEFGHIJKLM NOPQRSTUVWXY Z&£1234567890 ROCKWELL SHADOW (24-point)

ABCDEFGHIJKLMNOPQRS TUVWXYZ & £1234567890 abcdefghijklmnoprstuvwxyz ROCKWELL MEDIUM (24-point)

ABCDEFGHIJKLMNOPQRSTUVWXYZ abcdefghijklmnopqrstuvwxyz & £1234567890 MEMPHIS BOLD CONDENSED (24-point)

Examples of Egyptian typefaces advised as suitable for packaging.
From *Type in Advertising* by Alec Davies, 1951

comes to mind, yet the fact that it is in handwriting contributes to the effect as well. Davis was, however, rather more positive about the impact of certain typeface when he recommended 'Egyptian' –

'The wide use of Egyptian in packaging is partly due to their boxiness which seems to make them appropriate to wording on three-dimensional objects.'

Corvinus, designed in the 1930s, was, in fact, specifically designed for display. Coming in numerous versions in terms of weight and slant it was to be frequently used in packaging, along with Gill's Gill Sans (sans serifs), which had preceded it in 1928. Both were to serve packaging designers for some years in spite of being seen by some nervous manufacturers as too 'modern'.

ILLUSTRATION

Although biscuit tins, chocolate boxes and the like feature largely in the literature when it come to the historical use of surface illustration on packaging, illustration as an aspect of packaging design seems to have been of minor importance and is given slight attention in most of the text books on packaging. Obviously after the designer had laid out all the required information there would, in most cases, have been little space remaining for pictures. If an image appears at all on packaging over the period of this book it would tend to be the manufacturer's logo – Guinness's harp,

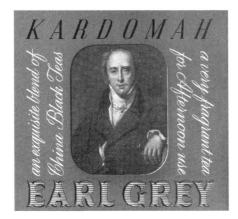

Jesse Collins designs for Kardomah teas, said to have sent sales 'shooting up', 1936

Left: Tin labels by W. Grimmond (top and bottom) and Horace Taylor (middle), *Commercial Art*, 1927

Right: Decorative headers from *Illustration* magazine, 1930s

HMV's dog, HP Sauce's Houses of Parliament, Kellogg's cockerel.

That early packaging bore few illustrations seems not only to have been related to limited space but to the quality of the material on which it was to be printed, which was often too rough to take much detail. When illustration began to appear it tended, as one writer put it, to be either 'pretty' or 'pompous' – women, children, cherubs, flora and fauna, or coats of arms and royalty. Typical were Alfred Munnings works, used occasionally for packaging from the time when he was apprenticed to the Norwich lithographers and box makers, Page Brothers, and Richard Cadbury's paintings of his daughter for his company's chocolate boxes. Max Beerbohm commented scathingly of such beauties – 'no discreet patron of the arts collects chocolate boxes'. Writing in the Penrose Annual of 1956, Alec Davis described the challenge for designers when it came to illustrations on packages –

> 'It was one of the hardest tasks for designers of the great clean-up of the 1930s to convince the manufacturer that he ought to remove from his packs the pictures of himself, his factory, his product and its hard- earned gold medals…'

Illustrations of contents did occasionally occur on labels, but only really came into their own with the arrival of colour photography in the 1930s, particularly used for labels for canned vegetables, fruits and fish, albeit Milner Gray mentions having to draw fruit for labels 'as healthy and luxurious as possible'. Attempts to use the works of celebrated artists for packaging – Cadbury's invitation to the likes of Laura Knight and CRW Nevinson for its boxes, or the Rothschild's use of Marie Laurencin, Henry Moore and Jean Cocteau for its bottle labels, was invariably unsuccessful and mostly illustrations, when they came to be used at all, were photographic.

VALIDATION

To complete a suitable packaging design, to have it accepted by all concerned, to get it into production and out on the market, was considered achievement enough, and that was that. But a few brave souls, mindful of a company's finances, began to ask was the expense worth it; where was the validation evidence? Often it was not possible to isolate the possible effect of the new packaging from everything else that was going on at the time, such as when it was part of a total company identity makeover, or had been allied with an advertising campaign. Over the period there seems to have been scant evidence that the cost of new packaging was more than offset by increased sales. When results were ever mentioned they tended to be vague and always optimistic; in the *Package Omnibus*, 1936, Jesse Collins' designs for Kardomah tea packs were said to have sent sales 'shooting up'.

By the mid-1930s several companies were looking to 'scientific' methods for validation of their outlay, not only for the finished packaging, but for each stage of its development, as when Rowntrees produced Black Magic. Some companies began to

WHATEVER YOU MAKE

—make a point of visiting this Exhibition at Olympia, London

ᐅᐅᐅᐅᐅᐅᐅᐅᐅᐅᐅᐅᐅᐅᐅ

MANUFACTURERS of every type of product, from cars to capsules, are faced with the problem of packaging — whether for Home or Export markets.

At THE PACKAGING EXHIBITION, over 150 of the leading members of the packaging industry show how the use of new developments in design, materials, methods and machinery can make *your* packaging pay—by reducing production costs and increasing sales at the point of purchase.

Everyone engaged in the marketing and selling of merchandise will find THE PACKAGING EXHIBITION interesting, stimulating and instructive.

Organised by
PROVINCIAL EXHIBITIONS LTD.

In association with
F. W. BRIDGES & SONS LTD.

In collaboration with The Institute of Packaging

REMEMBER
THE DATES
JAN 20th — 30th
1953

Open daily 10 a.m.—7 p.m.
(Except Sunday)

Packaging achieves exhibition status, *Sales Appeal*, 1953

ask users – retailers and customers – their opinions by interview and questionnaire or in focus groups; others resorted to such 'laboratory' tools as ocular cameras (to record eye movements), tachistoscopes (to test visual memory) and anglemeters (to record how a package is viewed from different positions).

An example of attempted validation was when designers McCann Product and Packaging Styling Services, designing for a well-known firm of manufacturing chemists, brought in the National Institute of Industrial Psychology (NIIP) to help them decide which, of some twelve possible packaging ideas to put forward to a client. A large representative sample of standard customers and some fifty retail chemists were asked to give immediate, and then, considered, opinions of mock-ups, including the then current design. Both chemists and customers came up with the same first choice, which the designers then felt was sufficiently validated to be put forward.

PROFESSIONALISM

Packaging design was slow to emerge as a design category, let alone a profession, lying as it does between product and graphic design. What commentary that did appear, even in specialised journals such as 'Shelf Appeal', tended to be critical of what was going on. Annuals, such as, the *Packaging Omnibus* were sprinkled with damnations –

Shelf Appeal a monthly publication 'Devoted to the planning, designing, manufacturing and display of the package.' On the left, claiming to be the first printed aluminium cover, designed by E McKnight Kauffer and on the right from a lino cut by Edward Bawden

the art of packaging

PACKAGE DESIGN

by Milner Gray R.D.I., F.S.I.A.

MASTER OF THE FACULTY OF ROYAL DESIGNERS FOR INDUSTRY

PAST PRESIDENT, SOCIETY OF INDUSTRIAL ARTISTS

BY D.E.A. CHARLTON

EDITOR OF MODERN PACKAGING

WITH CONTRIBUTIONS FROM

Kenneth Lamble, M.S.I.A.
C. W. Cousland, B.COMM. D.A.
A. F. Cowan
E. J. Gooding, B.SC., PH.D., S.S.G.T.
R. Hooper, M.S.I.A.

THE STUDIO PUBLICATIONS London & New York

Fundamentals

Published under the authority of the Council of the Institute of Packaging

of Packaging

Technical Editor F. A. PAINE B.Sc., F.R.I.C., M.Inst. Pkg.

BLACKIE & SON LIMITED London Glasgow

Three major packaging text books, *the art of packaging* by DEA Charlton, 1937, *Package Design* by Milner Gray, 1955 and *The Fundamentals of Packaging* by FA Paine, 1962

'*The average design for a moderate priced tea wrapper is out-of-date, completely lacking in selling power, ineffective in display…*'

Only occasionally were there glimmers of hope as when *Commercial Art*, in 1931, reported –

'*…hard-hearted gentlemen of industry are growing weaker and weaker in their resistance to clothing their products in gay appeal. Once they seemed to feel it rather undignified to place their sterling products in boxes and cartons and to package wares which for generations have been sold on their merit and in spite of their painfully unattractive appearance.*'

Other publications, not previously known for paying much attention to packaging, began to take note, as when the 1933 *Penrose Annual* declared –

'*a whole new field of work has opened up in the field of graphic arts by the growth in the use of packages, and it is a field which has not by any means yet reached its limits.*'

Progress in the growth of packaging design as a profession was put on hold by the onset of war. It was not until the immediate post-war years that the Institute of Packaging was

Cover for *Sales Appeal & Packaging Technology*, 1962

founded (1947) initially with its own headquarters, providing club facilities for members and putting on exhibitions. The Institute established standards and developed educational programmes with examinations; by the late 1950s there was an established qualified membership scheme.

Yet little was happening in the art colleges, which had hardly got round to recognising the need for product design courses, let alone packaging ones. An exception was Manchester Education authority which not only combined with the Institute, in 1961, to lay on a packaging conference at its College of Science and Technology, but offered a £500 Packaging Design Fellowship at its College of Art & Design.

Meanwhile specialist publications were beginning to appear. *Shelf Appeal*, which had been in existence prior to the war, was overtaken by *Sales Appeal* and similar titles – *The British Packer*, *Packaging*, the *Packer and Shipper*, (all based in London), along with the Manchester based *Packing Review*. *Packaging News* came on to the market in 1957 and by the mid-60s the Society of Industrial Artists newsletter described it as –

> '…the most comprehensive packaging newspaper in the world sent free to anyone concerned with companies' packaging policy/execution.'

When it came to textbooks the Americans, who were always a few steps ahead when it came to the technology and design of packaging, published an early 'bible' – DEA Charlton's 1937 *The Art of Packaging*. That many concerned in different ways with packaging were aware of its publication were the various hypes by William Crawford (advertising agent), F.N. Hepworth (Chairman of Metal Box), W.M. Larkins (of J.Walter Thompson), Norbert Dutton (then freelance) and Milner Gray in 1938 in *Art & Industry*, Crawford's being in his grandiose style –

> '*This book, by one of the most able exponents of the subject, comes at a momentous stage in the development of packaging. It reveals brilliantly the astonishing advances made in recent years.*'

The Institute did not bring out its *Fundamentals of Packaging* until 1962, some seven years after Britain's own packaging guru, Milner Gray, had published *Packaging Design*.

So, by the late 1960s, Britain had its own professional packaging design body, its own professional qualifications, a range of related journals, and all of this 'underwritten', as it were, by relevant research and proselytising emerging from the Printing, Packaging & Allied Trades Research Association at Leatherhead. The newly formed Design Council also offered support by laying on exhibitions and offering space for members of Society of Industrial Artists (SIA) to show off their work in packaging, which, for example, Hans Schleger took up with his designs for the British Sugar Corporation.

SKILLS AND ROLES OF A PACKAGING DESIGNER

From all that has come before in this book it will be clear that a full-blooded package designer, i.e. one designing the package itself as well as its surface, needs to be something of a polymath, alert to developments in a range of disciplines impinging on possible solutions – engineering (the machinery needed for making/filling/sealing); chemistry and physics (the qualities of the packaging material and the contents to be packed); psychology and sociology (to understand consumers' attitudes and behaviours); economics and finance (to take into consideration budgeting and marketing); oh! just as an after thought – and all the skills of a graphic designer.

Some would add to this the skills of a diplomat. Perhaps the majority of package designers just wanted to get their noses down, focus on their briefs, and get the job done within the time limit. But others have rebelled against just doing what they were told, and wanted to ask questions, some of which could well affect the way a client was operating. SIA appears to have gone along with this more energetic approach to commissions –

> *'the more responsibility the designer is willing and able*
> *to accept, the greater will be the contribution he makes*
> *to his client's prosperity.'*

The meek, reactive, packaging designer was to become an activist!

Arrival of modernism in packaging design, 1936

WRAPPING CHOCOLATE

Although chocolate, in the form of beans, is thought to have arrived in England as early as 1650, its popularity was as a drink; chocolate to be eaten only came on the scene some centuries later when Fry's of Bristol moulded what has claimed to be the first recognizable chocolate bar, in 1847.

Fry, an apothecary, had set up shop in 1753, but it was his son, also Joseph, who succeeded him in 1795, who was to grow the business into becoming the major British chocolate manufacturer of the 19th century. Fry's main competitors were John Cadbury of Birmingham, establishing his business in 1824 (to be succeeded by his sons Richard and

Cadbury's Chocolate Buttons
Sales Appeal, 1961

George), and Henry Rowntree of York, who had purchased his then employer's cocoa, chocolate and chicory business in 1862. Of course there were also the Europeans, the French and the Swiss, the elite of the industry, only really dislodged to any extent from this position when imports were blocked in WWI.

The Fry's, Cadbury's and Rowntree's were all Quakers, sharing common values and friendship, focusing, at times, as much interest and energy on the welfare of their employees and communities as on the profitability of their products. The relationship between the three was paradoxical in that they were competitors, but, when they saw a matter that would be of mutual advantage, they would cooperate, as when Cadbury's and Fry's, from time

Opposite: Wrapping paper by Shep for Carsons Chocolates, 1924

War–time rationing of paper and print led Fry's to overstamp old labels and wrappings

to time would buy beans in bulk together. The three came to meet regularly in Cheltenham to settle between themselves such matters as, or instance, pricing and promotions; even, in WWII, committing themselves to helping each other out if any were bombed. Terry's, also of York, stood apart from the Quaker trio, but was later to function, as the others, as a competitor and confederate, joining the Cheltenham meetings. Cadbury's was perhaps the sharpest of the group commercially, continually undercutting on prices, and eventually absorbing and nearly obliterating Fry's.

Initially chocolates were sold loose, by weight, displayed on trays, as well as in bars and boxes. Later bars would be

The evolution of Cadbury's Dairy Milk, progressivley simplified and with the introduction of the Cadbury's signature. The last version was designed by Norbert Dutton in,1951

displayed in glass cases, which although preventing pilfering also prevented much impulse buying being encased, the cases coming to be known in the trade as 'coffins'. As, in newspaper shops and confectioners, chocolates from the different manufacturers often came to be displayed together, the wrapping became increasingly important to distinguish the brands.

Chocolate, as a commodity, is sensitive to moisture and heat, milk chocolate more so than plain. Fry's were noted as particularly scrupulous in seeing that their women packers hands were sufficiently cool each morning before they started their work. But it was Fry's that tripped up, when it came to vulnerability, when its Crunchie bar, hyped for the sharp snapping sound when it was bitten, was found not to do so when the initial wrapping proved insufficiently watertight. When new wrapping was introduced Fry's thought it necessary to have 'watertight' printed on it. Moisture and heat were obviously of even more crucial concern when chocolate was being exported to hot climes, Terry's, for example, taking extra care, packing their export chocolate in tins.

Packaging became even more important when bars came to be laid out in the open in retailers, often near the till. Instances are given of customers complaining that other hands, particularly those of school children, might have left contaminating marks on the wrappers when deciding which to buy. As with so much packaging, customers became loyal to recognisable chocolate brands, and were wont to comment as to possible loss of quality or weight of the chocolate within if changes were made to the look of the wrapping.

Above: An early 'Puginesque' wrapper for Fry's Chocolate Cream, 1875
Below: The modern version pared down to basics with Fry's name dominant, 1960s

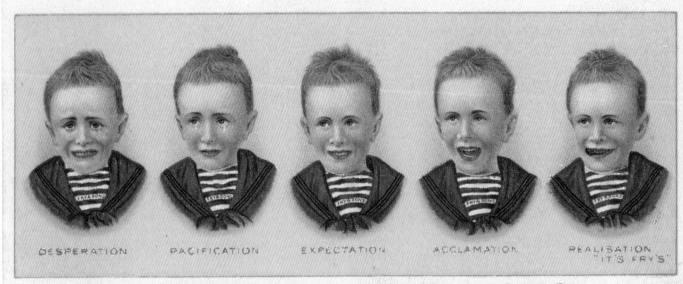

A postcard for the much promoted Five Boys chocolate, 1920s

Postcards for Fry's Five Boys chocolate and Cocoa, 1920s

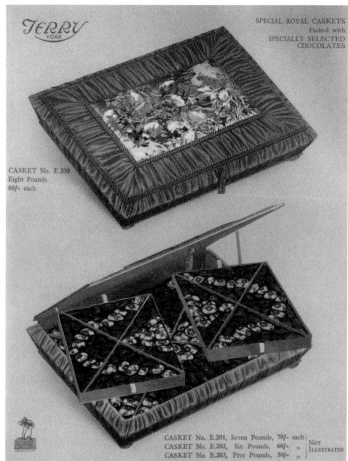

Early Terry's packaging for chocolate apples and oranges
and Special Royal Caskets

Above: Rowntree's 1930 box with photographs of contents on the lid
Below: Leonard Beaumont's elegant designs for Nestlé

When it came to chocolate bars, Fry's initially dominated the market, with its Chocolate Cream, Five Boys, and Turkish Delight, all launched successfully before WWI. Cadbury's and Fry's, continually at war, each resorted to giving their bars Swiss related names as 'Alpina' and 'Mountain' to suggest a higher quality than that of their competitor. In 1905, Cadbury's got an edge with its highly successful Dairy Milk, to be followed shortly by Bournville. Into the 1920s Cadbury's seemed to have a ceaseless flow of new products of pocket size, including Crème Eggs, Flake, and Fruit and Nut. Rowntree's was late to the 'bar' market but had its triumphs in the 1930s with Kit Kat and Aero. Then came the arrival of the American, Mars, and even Terry's, who usually sold its chocolates loose or boxed, produced its Chocolate Orange. Mars was to win a considerable share of this market in the post-war years with its Bounty, Galaxy and Twix.

As choosing a chocolate bar became increasingly a matter of self-service, the wrappers were crucial and colour was a main distinguishing factor. Printing in colour was expensive and for bars one colour was usually resorted to, and at the most two. Cadbury's chose a regal purple and gold, and customers soon learnt to pick out, immediately, the red of Kit Kat, the reddish purple of Turkish Delight, the brown of Mars bars, the gold of Crunchie, and the blue and white of Chocolate Cream, although shape and size would also have been a factor.

Generally wrappers on bars would have only carried the manufacturer's and the brand name, the weight, and, in the early years, the price. Illustration was rarely used except in the case

An in house designer and women in the packing department and
opposite packing by hand from a chart at Cadbury's, 1930s

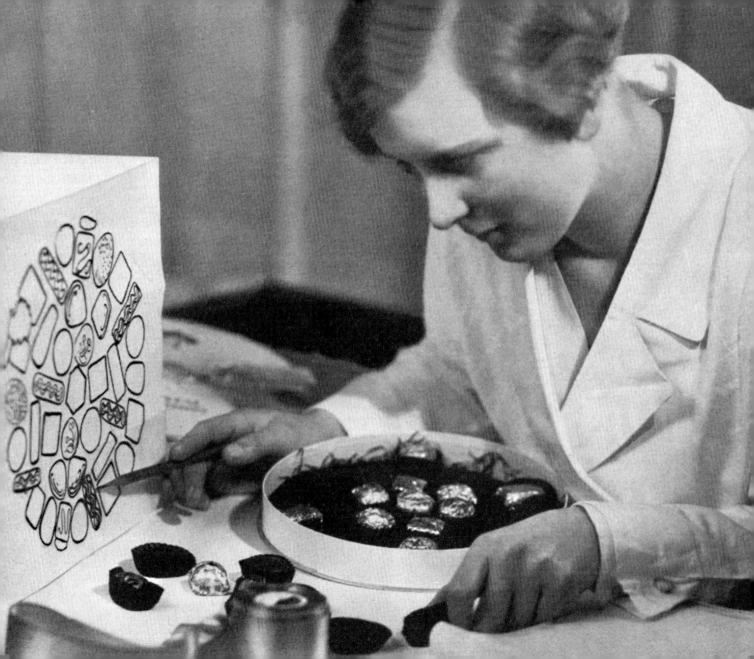

of Five Boys (images of an American boy that Conrad Fry had bought up 'just in case'); and then, after WWII, Cadbury's 'glass and a half' on its milk chocolate bar. Whether the manufacturer's or the brand's name was the most prominent seems to have been related either to the egos of the families involved or, more importantly, the state of the market. After Cadbury's had virtually taken over Fry's it determined that the Fry's name would only appear on what would prove to be its most profitable products.

Cadbury's name always dominated on its packaging, until, somewhat late in the day, it realised that competitors were selling by brand name. Cadbury's had considered its name so key as a selling point that, in 1921, it had had the typography done as a signature, said to be that of the founder of the firm. And there it remained even when, in 1941, Norbert Dutton was brought in to redesign the wrappings, cutting away the curlicues etc. yet leaving the signature. Yet over the same period most consumers would not have bothered noticing who, precisely, were the manufacturers of Kit Kat, Aero or Crunchie, whose selling point was their brand name.

Billy Butlin had stressed that an idea should be good before it was wrapped in cellophane, and the various chocolate manufacturers began to understand that unless a new product offered something original, no amount of clever colourful wrapping would ensure its success. Fry's, at its lowest period, in a desperate attempt to survive, flooded the market with what it hoped were potential winners, largely coming from the imaginations of its directors or manufacturing departments, most

of which died a quick death. Rowntree's, too, had periods which can only be described as random product development in a 'suck it and see' mode, finding that a large number of its so attractively wrapped products turned out to be flops.

Boxed chocolates needed special consideration when it came to packaging, as a box of chocolates was expensive, and for a long time purchased only by the well-off, or for very special occasions. In the early years, a gift of a box of chocolates could even have the significance of a marriage proposal possibly being on its way. And throughout the period 'special' boxes were issued for such events as coronations and key wedding celebrations, suitably wrapped in silver, gold, whatever.

The packers of chocolate boxes were highly valued and often closely supervised. Packers were nearly always women, said to be chosen for the slenderness of their fingers, so suitable for such a delicate task! A cynic might add that as labour was the most expensive production cost, women could be employed more cheaply. Each day nails and hair would be checked before the packers got to work, in the early years standing to their task, with only short breaks in the morning and afternoon. They were usually paid by piece rate and if any instance of slovenly packing occurred the packer was suspended for the day, therefore losing wages. At Terry's the packers were numbered and a numbered ticket was placed in each box so that checks could be made.

How the box was to be decorated was always a crucial decision. So important was each new design that when, in 1952, a Fry's employee leaked its proposed Coronation

'Jazz Age' box label for Cadbury's Mayfair Chocolates by Austin Cooper, 1929

Richard Cadbury's portraits of his daughter Jessie

Commemorative design to a competitor, the treachery made the national press. In the 19th century and into the 20th, chocolate manufacturers tended to buy in sheets of pictures from printers for box decoration, but as early as the 1860s Cadbury's advertised –

'Messrs. Cadbury's box of chocolate crème is among the pictorial novelties offered to the trade. Chaste yet simple, it consists of a blue-eyed maiden some

six summers old… designed and drawn by Mr. Richard Cadbury.'

The 'blue-eyed maiden' was Jessie, Richard's daughter. Having made the decision to design his company's chocolate boxes, Richard was soon turning out decorative flowers, trees, alpine scenes and the like. However, when Cadbury's produced its highly successful Milk Tray, in 1915, it settled on an altogether

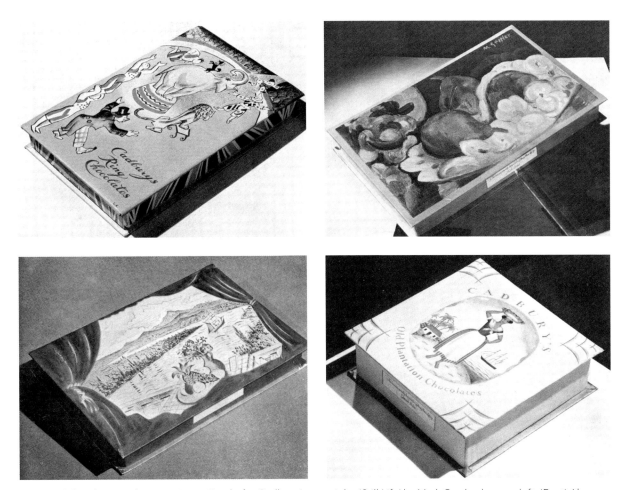

Top left, 'The Ring' by Dame Laura Knight for Cadbury's, top right, 'Still Life' by Mark Gertler, bottom left, 'Exotic' by CRW Nevinson, bottom right, 'Old Plantation' by Edmund Dulac for Cadbury's, 1933

Advertisment designed by Gilroy for Rowntree's, 1928. Chocolate boxes, being expensive, tended to be gifts that suggested a marriage proposal was on it's way.

plainer affair. Advertised as 'the box for the pocket' and meant for a mass market, its simple design barely changed for decades ahead.

By the 1930s Cadbury's had its own art department which produced designs for standard product packaging and for specials, as for Christmas, for which, often, dozens of designs would be considered before one was settled upon. Yet the company seems not to have been totally satisfied with what was emerging from its own studio when it came to box design, for it ran an open competition with an extraordinary prize of one hundred guineas. The response was enormous, and from the two hundred short-listed a Miss Judy Shaw won with an oriental willow pattern, hardly the epitome of the modernism that was the rage at that time.

This, perhaps, not proving the most useful way of finding a 'winner' Cadbury's then, in 1933, turned to 'fine' artists as a possible resource, those so commissioned included Mark Gertler, Laura Knight and CRW Nevinson, and the illustrators Edmond Dulac and Arthur Rackham. The results again proved disappointing, as none of those invited really understood the way a chocolate box was seen and handled. Gertler's offering, for example, was done on canvas, a rough large surface, which then had to be reproduced on a smooth small one. The company salvaged what it could by displaying these artists' works at the Leicester Galleries, which no doubt provided some kind of kudos to the company.

When Cadbury's came up with its mixed boxed assortment,

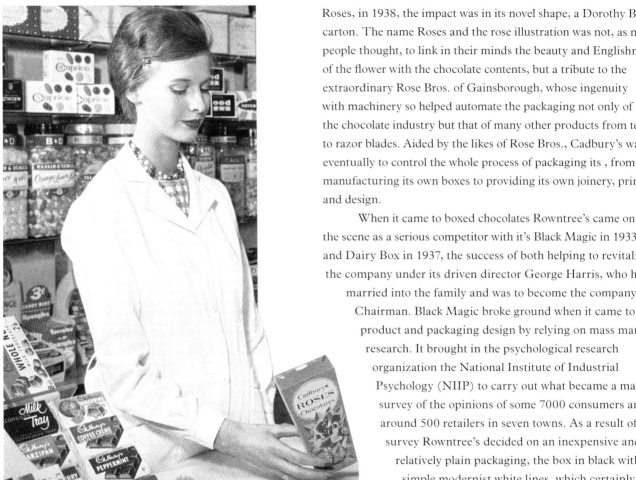

Cadbury's innovative carton for Roses, 1962

Roses, in 1938, the impact was in its novel shape, a Dorothy Bag carton. The name Roses and the rose illustration was not, as most people thought, to link in their minds the beauty and Englishness of the flower with the chocolate contents, but a tribute to the extraordinary Rose Bros. of Gainsborough, whose ingenuity with machinery so helped automate the packaging not only of the chocolate industry but that of many other products from tea to razor blades. Aided by the likes of Rose Bros., Cadbury's was eventually to control the whole process of packaging its , from manufacturing its own boxes to providing its own joinery, printing and design.

When it came to boxed chocolates Rowntree's came on the scene as a serious competitor with it's Black Magic in 1933 and Dairy Box in 1937, the success of both helping to revitalise the company under its driven director George Harris, who had married into the family and was to become the company's Chairman. Black Magic broke ground when it came to product and packaging design by relying on mass market research. It brought in the psychological research organization the National Institute of Industrial Psychology (NIIP) to carry out what became a massive survey of the opinions of some 7000 consumers and around 500 retailers in seven towns. As a result of the survey Rowntree's decided on an inexpensive and relatively plain packaging, the box in black with simple modernist white lines, which certainly distinguished it from all the flowery boxes then

Black Magic from market research by NIIP, 1955

on the market. The box design and the name was to become iconic as a brand image; the NIIP psychologist whose market research was not only responsible for this success but also for the brands Kit Kat and Aero, went on to achieve fame as the novelist and film script writer Nigel Balchin. By the time I, myself, was working for NIIP in the 1950s, our work for Black Magic had become an organisational legend.

The actual packing of chocolates into the Black Magic boxes was reported as backbreaking, particularly the placing of the more intricately shaped chocolates as the crescent coffee creams. Initially the separate chocolates would arrive on wooden trays and the packers would have to reach up for them, but later things were made easier by the introduction of conveyor belts. Rowntree's was to use black again with its post-WWII boxes of After Eight, black by then had become accepted as the epitome of sophistication, suggestive of smart dinner parties rounding up with coffee, digestifs and chocolates.

Although the names Fry's, Cadbury's Rowntree's and Terry's have survived and are still appearing on packaging, the companies themselves have been sold, sold again, merged, and swallowed. Fry's, Cadbury's, and Terry's became part of Kraft Foods, Rowntree's part of Nestlé. The various packaging, in red, gold, blue and white, orange, purple and black, as the companies' names, still serve to distinguish the brands and, consequently, still seem crucial to maintaining consumer loyalty.

THE REST OF THE STORY
There are two reasons why Black Magic chocolates are worth writing home about. First, those really *luscious* centres. And then, however much you pay, you won't find *better* chocolates than Black Magic. This is because Rowntrees put all the value into the chocolates themselves, packing them simply, but elegantly, in a smart black box.

Illustrated advertisment by 'Eric' (Carl Erickson), 1953

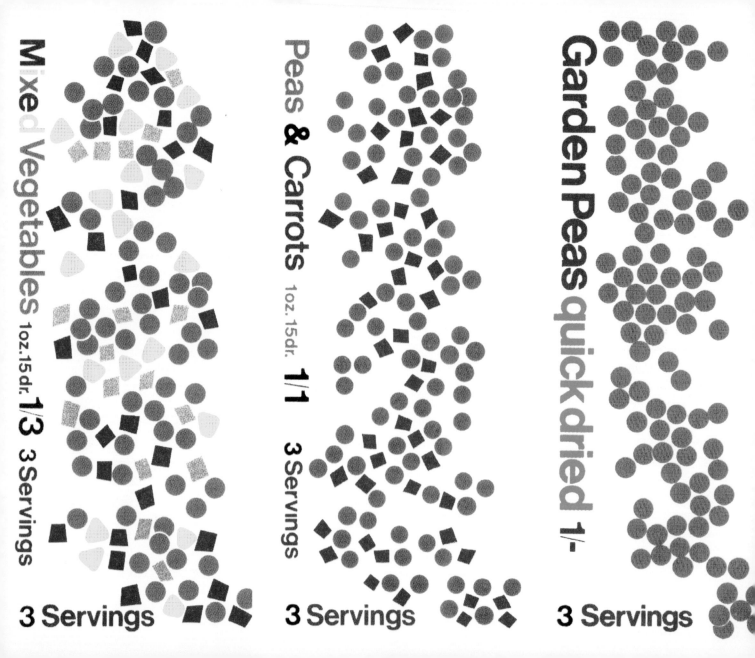

Mixed Vegetables 1oz.15dr. 1/3 3 Servings

3 Servings

Peas & Carrots 1oz.15dr. 1/1 3 Servings

3 Servings

Garden Peas quick dried 1/-

3 Servings

OWN BRAND PACKAGING

'Overlooking Blackfriars Bridge and the barges chugging up and down the Thames, five men in a studio at the top of Stamford House, the headquarters of J.Sainsbury... work in close harmony and often at the pace of the men just across the river in Fleet Street.'

This was the start of an article in an SIA newsletter in 1964 announcing the setting up of the Sainsbury's own studio, and describing its work on packaging for its new own-brand range.

The growth of Sainsbury's is one of many 'rags-to-riches' stories of the entrepreneurial Victorian age. In 1869 a picture framer John James Sainsbury married Mary Ann, the daughter of a St. Pancras dairyman, and the pair set up shop in Drury Lane selling butter, eggs and milk – products which future generations of Sainsbury men would own as of their direct interest in growing the company. It was the couples son, John, who was to expand the business, developing a chain of grocery shops across the country; and his son, Alan, who, inspired by a visit to the United States, who claimed to have brought the concept of self-service to Britain, converting Sainsbury's Croydon branch from its conventional counter service in 1950. This involved Sainsbury's in some own-product branding, long before the studio, of the SIA article, was established. For this Alan Sainsbury used an external designer, Leonard Beaumont, who was to act as the company's design consultant for all its 'visuals' for some fourteen years.

Leonard Beaumont, a highly talented and versatile artist, but now largely forgotten, was nearing sixty when starting his Sainsbury projects. Born and brought up in Sheffield, he began his art training in evening classes, whilst working on advertisements for the Sheffield Daily Telegraph. Eventually he obtained a scholarship, which enabled him to study full-time at the local art school before returning to work on the newspaper, becoming its art director in 1933. Beyond the walls of his workplace Beaumont developed his skills in printmaking, working along similar lines, and to as high a standard, as was being produced by Cyril Power and Sybil Andrews of the Grosvenor School.

It is not recorded how Beaumont came to the notice of Francis Meynell, the distinguished private press publisher, but it was Meynell who induced him to come to London, in 1936, to

Opposite: Sainsbury's own label dried vegetables, 1970s

Leonard Beaumont for Sainsbury's. Own brand designs using Bethold Wolpe's Albertus typeface, 1954

Leonard Beaumont's Sainsbury's own brand flavoured jelly cubes, 1954

Herbs and spices in cardboard drums, Leonard Beaumont for Sainbury's

become Art Director for the Publicity Department of United Artists Film Distributors, responsible for its poster work. From this Beaumont moved on to join the advertising agents Mather & Crowther as Head of Design and it was from this base that he was commissioned by Sainsbury's.

Alan Sainsbury nostalgically recalled the spruceness of his grandparents establishment in Drury Lane, with its marble-topped counters and tiled floors and walls, and this was in his mind when he briefed Beaumont. He was later to declare –

'We have well-designed packaging and point-of-sale material because it gives the right impression of cleanliness and tidiness.'

In his dislike of frills and fussiness Sainsbury was also much influenced by the discipline and simplification that Frank Pick was bringing to all the visual aspects of London Transport.

Beaumont, who had actually done some work for the company before WWII, was now used for a very wide range of Sainsbury assignments from shop fascia to invoice forms, practically a total corporate reimaging. Initially, with rationing still in operation until 1954, the development of 'own brand' products was limited, but with the end of rationing and the expansion of self-service it became essential for 'own brand' to stand out from its competitors. Sainsbury's took on the challenge for a large number of products down to the humble packaging of Sainsbury's ground white pepper! Beaumont was sympathetic to Alan Sainsbury's preference for simplicity and discipline, describing his years working for the company as 'bringing order out of chaos'. For this Beaumont's inclination was to have the colour white predominate in his packaging design –

'The purity of white, along with clear consistent graphics, evoked a confidence in the mind of the shopper.'

At first working with paper and cardboard, he was soon to be challenged by such plastics as polythene and cellulose. He not only redesigned for 'own brand' goods that already had packaging, providing surface graphics, but actually designed the packaging itself for goods, such as eggs, which had previously been sold loose.

It was Beaumont, by then in his 70s, who suggested that Sainsbury's set up its own internal design unit. Although he retired in 1964, he built a kind of friendship with the appointed head of the new unit, Peter Dixon, visiting him from time to time to complain about any design faults he had found in his local Sainsbury store.

Peter Dixon could be described as a jobbing designer with his feet well grounded. He escaped the rarified aesthetics of art schools (at the time his major interest had been with sport), and received his training through an apprenticeship supplemented by studies at the London College of Printing. After a period of National Service (1947-50), he worked in the design offices of a number of firms including Clark's Shoes and Wiggins Teape, the latter providing him with a sound understanding of paper and paper products, so central to packaging design. In that the studio at Blackfriars came to consist of a mix of art school and apprentice trained designers it might be said to have had the potential for both original but practical solutions to packaging problems.

It was Alan Sainsbury's son John Davan (JD) who completely rid the firm of counter service and hugely expanded the self-service stores. JD was much the same age as Dixon and came into the company as a buyer, but a buyer with strong artistic

Sainbury's 1960s bold sans-serif applied to carry home cartons

Left, a 1970 in house design, right, a rare subcontracted design to an ex fellow LCP student of Peter Dixon

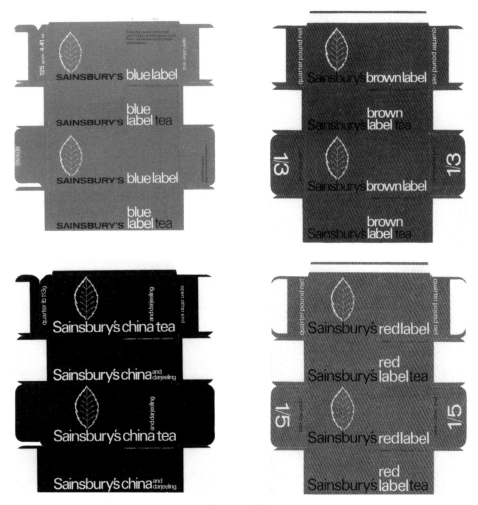

In house designs for own label tea range, 1965

interests, ranging from gallery visiting and hanging fine art in his office, to, later on, with his brother, funding a new wing for the National Gallery and making donations to the British Museum. He and Dixon bonded and, indeed, both were to retire within a few years of each other. JD was committed to design and Dixon to Sainsbury's business policy, which brought an empathy and synergy to their working together.

JD was much given to somewhat pious pronouncements on Sainsbury's ethics as with –

'Most people went into private label to get a cheap line; they were only concerned with price. But as well as the price advantage, we were concerned with matching or improving of the quality of the brand leader.'

and –

'The philosophy of the design was to make it easy and clear. It was our responsibility to understand the customer's needs and inform her on every aspect of what she was buying.'

JD was to claim that he aimed to get good design by giving freedom to the designer, and it seems disagreements between him and Dixon were rare. But in reality, Dixon must, at times, have been constrained if not frustrated. In obituaries JD is described

as 'forceful and autocratic' and, indeed, insisted on approving every 'own label' design, which suggests a rather less than liberal management style. And then, of course, as with every 'own-label' packaging designer, there were the attitudes of the company's buyers and of the sourcing manufacturers to be taken into account.

The buyers were the ones to purchase goods that it had been decided should become 'own label', and often these products came with the related packaging and printing of the manufacturer. All parties would have had their opinions on the repackaging which, no doubt, at times, were entrenched, the buyer concerned with consumer and marketing aspects, the manufacturer with consumer loyalty to the product as it was, the printer alert to the cost and difficulty of any radical change. All this could well have left Dixon and his team with little room for originality and much need for compromise; it was up to Dixon to argue his team's corner.

It was generally agreed that the company's name should be prominent and set in Venus Bold Extended type, although Dixon would be free to use other typeface for additional wording on the package for content, weight and price. The only disagreement JD and Dixon seem to have had over words on packaging was that JD disliked typography at an angle which Dixon preferred for its energy. For items such as fruit and vegetables, Dixon would include an illustration in his design. His use of colour was restrained and mainly used for distinguishing families of products within a brand.

Dixon's style has often been described as along Bauhaus lines, although, it is thought that as a jobbing designer Dixon

Verging on Pop Art, a selection of 1970s own label crisp packets.

Frozen foods range, 1960s

Packet soups, 1973

was largely unaware or uninfluenced by the philosophy of design movements. By the late 1960s well over 300 products had been given Sainsbury's own-label packaging, largely designed by the studio, although occasionally Dixon would farm out illustrative work, as for the sun on the cornflake packages, which went to an ex-fellow student from the London College of Printing.

An image of Dixon and his team inundated with packaging briefs to be done to tight deadlines (along with all the other demands on them for advertising and publicity), with JD standing over his shoulder, is, perhaps, something of a caricature, for not infrequently he went out to visit the Sainsbury stores, to inspect the displays, and to watch actual customer behavior, in order to get feedback and new ideas.

In his introduction to 'Own Label' Johny Trunk, an enthusiast for the studios' work, summed up the fifteen years of its output to 1977 as –

'a striking experimental modernity which pushed the boundaries, reflecting a period of optimism, and helping Sainsbury's into a brand giant.'

Macdonalds

GLENGARRY

GLENGARRY

Macdonalds

WILLIAM MACDONALD & SONS (BISCUITS) LIMITED

GLENGARRY BISCUIT BAKERY HILLINGTON GLASGOW

PACKAGING DESIGNERS

'My father was a dab hand at doing up parcels, we would stand by and admire the skillful fold of paper and deft knotting of string... whether this may have influenced me in later years I leave to the psychologists' **Milner Gray address to the Double Crown Club – 'A Brave Lot O'String' 1956**

Packaging designers come in all shapes and sizes – they have been employed full-time by the manufacturers of packaging materials – Metal Box, Bowaters, de la Rue – all had their own studios; they may have worked in design/artists studios which offered package design along with a myriad of other design services – for instance Carlton, Clement Dane, Norfolk, Reimann or the Industrial Design Partnership; or actually running their own studios as FHK Henrion or Hans Schleger; they could have been employed by advertising agencies – Ashley Havinden with Crawfords and Ruth Gill with Colman, Prentis & Varley, perhaps taking on a packaging assignment riding on an advertising one; they might be employed in the studios of a large retail chain, as Sainsbury's or Marks & Spencer, putting out 'own-brand' packaging; or then, again, they might just have been a 'fine' artist or illustrator whose work had inadvertently strayed

into the world of commerce – as Barnett Freedman providing designs for Glengarry biscuits. This section will explore some of the personalities working in the field of 'wrapping and packaging' starting with the guru of British packaging design – Milner Gray.

MILNER GRAY AND HIS DESIGN ASSOCIATES

Milner Gray was a towering figure in mid-20th century British design – he wrote or was written about in dozens of design publications, and beyond these his name was wont to appear in such nationals as The Times; he penned, or co-authored books and wrote chapters in others; he taught, examined or was on the board of some ten art colleges (becoming principal of Sir John Cass School of Arts & Crafts) and served on committees on art education; he spoke at numerous society meetings and conferences

Opposite: Glengarry biscuits design by Barnett Freedman, 1940s

both in Britain and abroad; he was a founder member of a major designer society (SIAD) and of one of the most influential design groups, (DRU); he was design consultant to a dozen or so companies; he served the country during WWII as Head of the Ministry of Information Exhibition Branch; he was honoured with an OBE; and in his career he designed textiles, murals, chairs, silverware, exhibitions, trade marks, interiors, armorial bearings and PACKAGING. It is true he lived to nearly one hundred but he can be said not to have wasted a minute!

It is recorded that Gray was a sickly child, thrown back on his own resources. His later independent views may well have stemmed from this but he certainly did not work in isolation as an adult, a creative artist ploughing his lonely furrow in his studio. Gray was someone who realised much design needed many heads and hands, albeit he invariably preferred to be the leader of the group. In *Art & Industry*, in 1950, George Butler, the then art director of the advertising agency J.Walter Thompson, wrote of Gray as –

> *'…one of the first to realise that many modern designing tasks are beyond the power of the individual artist working alone and can best be tackled by a small group of diverse specialists working together on a more or less equal footing was Milner Gray.'*

This realisation came to Gray when he was barely out of college for, in 1921, after leaving Goldsmiths where he had studied art and design, he and some of his fellow students formed the Bassett-Gray Group of Artists & Writers, offering design services for posters, advertisements, symbols and other graphics (packaging being included in the Group's advertisements); and working on general consultancy assignments largely in the china industry. After a certain amount of coming and going the Group was re-organised in 1935 as the Industrial Design Partnership (IDP) with Gray as the senior partner. Among the very varied commissions he undertook, Gray began to build up a sort of reputation for packaging design in particular. In 1935 the *Boxmakers Journal & Packaging Review* recorded –

> *'The group is equipped through its research and the specialised knowledge of one or several of its members, to give intelligent assistance and guidance to any firm that sees the value of a good pack in the selling scheme.'*

Gray had already begun to write on the subject of packaging as in an article in *Commercial Art* in 1934, entitled 'Shape, Design & Colour of the Package', based on his work with a number of firms including Hartley's (canned fruit) and Smith's Crisps; and, in 1938 he addressed the Royal Society of Arts on 'The History and Development of Packaging'.

At the onset of war Gray's IDP was closed; but before the end of the war a new design group was being hatched that was to morph into the iconic Design Research Unit, headed by Gray and Misha Black (who had worked with him at IDP).

*We believe that there is no bet-ter way of selling your goods than that we design them

*
MISHA BLACK   JESSE COLLINS   MILNER GRAY
THOMAS GRAY   DE HOLDEN STONE   WALTER LANDAUER
INDUSTRIAL DESIGN PARTNERSHIP · 4 BEDFORD SQ., LONDON, W.C.1 · MUSEUM 4307-8
Publicity Design · Window Display · Exhibition Architecture · Pakaging · Styling

Advertisment for the Industrial Design Partnership, mid 1930s

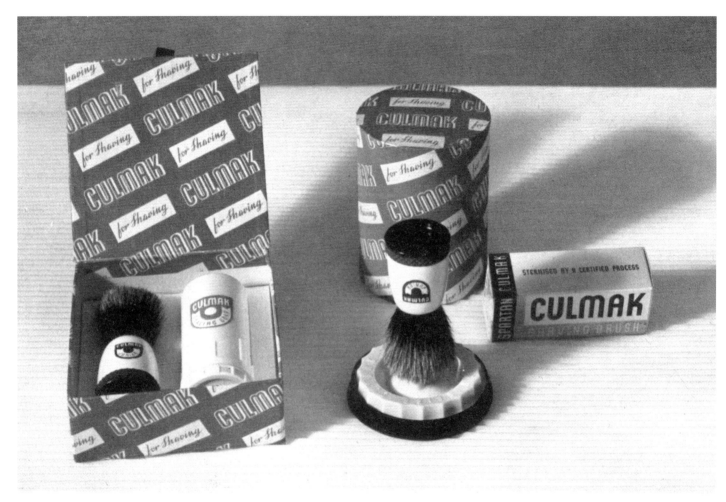

One of the last packaging designs from the Industrial Design Partnership for TW Culmer & Sons Ltd, 1939/40

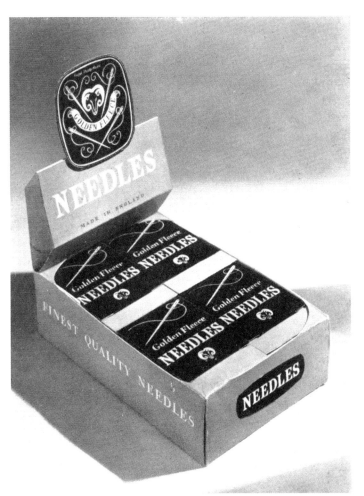

Milner Gray packaging for Needles Industries Ltd, 1940s

Milner Gray beer bottle labels for Courage & Co. Ltd, 1950s

In the 1950s and 60s Grays name was appearing continuously in the design press for a variety of projects including his packaging work for the Mid-Sussex Canning Preserve Co., the Rolex Watch Company and Tate & Lyle. By 1955 his packaging experience was such that he felt sufficiently confident to put his ideas on the subject into what became a textbook *Packaging Design*. In this he not only placed packaging design firmly within a company's marketing activities, but raised it from surface graphics to a matter of serious research, problem solving and validation – 'design is a process of analysis, synthesis and genesis'. Well abreast of the technical as well as the aesthetic aspects of packaging design Gray had already noted in an article in the *Penrose Annual* for 1940 that –

> *'designing for machine production has this difference from designing for handicraft, that it calls for not manipulative but for mental fecundity.'*

In an address to the Royal Society of Arts in 1959 he summarised his opinions on the necessary talents of a designer –

> *'He should be a creative artist, an experienced technician and a good organiser. He should be sensitive to the trends in world fashion. He should have the personality to get his opinions a hearing at management level; and the courage to fight his convictions.'*

And, indeed, much of Gray's packaging design, in the post-war years, was initiated at board level as part of his many corporate identity assignments, which could include anything from the look of buildings and delivery vans to how products were packed. Along with Grays memorable work for Ilford and Kodak, were make-overs for the drinks companies Gilbey's, Courage and Watney-Mann, and for the packaging material firms British Aluminium and de la Rue. His versatility and deep interest in the whole business of 'wrapping it up' even led him to invent a bottle-filling and capping machine for United Dairies.

Although Gray could be as 'modern' as any 'modernist' in his packaging design, a thread of his youthful interest in historical illustration seemed to have remained with him, occasionally emerging for such products as labels for drinks bottles. However the actual stretch of his historical interests, from the Middle Ages to the most up-to-date, showed itself in the wide ranging book he penned with Ronald Armstrong in 1962, *Lettering for Architects and Designers*.

For a good deal of his packaging design Gray was given sole accreditation, but for much of his 'packaging within corporate identity' schemes DRU colleagues and others, outside the unit, had their names alongside his – his package ranges for Ilford are also credited to Ronald Ingles and Joseph Revil; for Courage he worked with Peter Moro amongst others; whilst for Gilbey's he worked with a whole team from DRU including Kenneth Lamble.

Although Kenneth Lamble's name appears along with Grays, and occasionally on its own, when it comes to packaging,

Milner Gray packaging for rice with a lid as a measure, 1959

he seems a somewhat shadowy personality with little recorded about him. Before he joined DRU he worked as a glass designer and was to become a lecturer at Hornsey College of Art. Joining DRU, when it took on a large number of people for its work for the Festival of Britain, Lamble eventually became a partner. His interests in packaging extended beyond the work of the DRU to his becoming a member of the Society of Industrial Artist's Packaging Group Committee in the 1960s. He penned a rare note (rare for him) on the subject for the SIA's newsletter in 1963 where

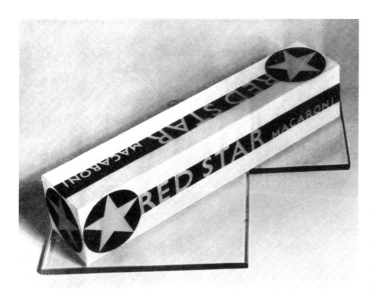

Alan Rogers of Bassett Gray designs for macaroni pack, 1934/5

he not only put over Gray's message of the rounded designer, but wrote optimistically of packaging design as evolving from 'just an extension of graphic and publicity design' to 'nearly a profession in its own right'.

Other DRU designers working alongside Gray but on their own commissions as well, were Jesse Collins, Peter Ray and Norbert Dutton. Jesse Collins was a stalwart – he had been with Gray from the days of the Industrial Design Partnership and is described as a founder member of the DRU. With IDP he had made something of a stir with his well-received packaging for Kardomah Tea, which, in the 1936 Omnibus of Marketing and Packaging was declared to have 'increased sales considerably'. When Charlton, the American designer, brought out his textbook *The Art of Packaging* in 1937, these designs were considered of sufficient merit to be included. Collins was to continue the tea interest in his commission for the Tea Bureau in the early 1950s, but he also worked on packaging for other goods, including Rothman's Cigarettes, Windsor & Newton's art materials and Idris drinks. Whilst at IDP Collins had also designed a sans serif alphabet specifically for commercial use, including on packaging, when few other suitable alphabets were available. Although Collins made some interesting contributions to the packaging industry he is altogether better remembered for the avant garde graphics department he built up at Central School of Arts and Crafts, described in the design press as 'a power house of creativity and experimentation'.

Yet another of Gray's DRU colleagues whose name was often linked to his when it came to packaging, was Peter Ray. Although Ray had tackled some packaging design prior to WWII he is perhaps best remembered for his post-war work for the Kingston department store Bentall's. In an article in *Art & Industry* in 1946 Ray places packaging design central to the government and industry's concern to rebuild British exports after the war –

'In addition to enhancing the reputation of both the product and the manufacturer the resulting packs

Milner Gray label designs for Hartley's tinned fruits, 1934

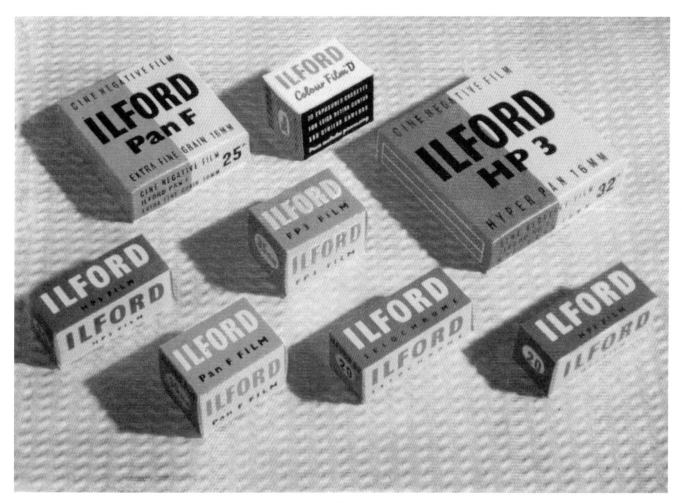

Milner Gray colour coding for Ilford photographic films, 1950s

Kenneth Lamble packaging for the Ilford Pixie camera, 1965

Kenneth Lamble (Illustration Joyce Bowman) see-through carry home pack for a waistcoat, 1958

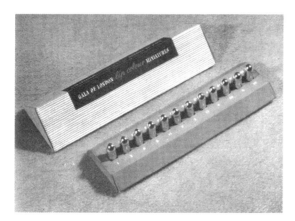

Kenneth Lamble clever packaging for Gala Lipstick, 1951

will sell the goods in increasing numbers, and the manufacturer will be able to compete for export markets with the confidence that goes with the knowledge that his packages have the atmosphere of the products they contain, and, even more important, they look British.'

Ray, swept up into the post-war drive to rebuild the economy, through the auspices of SIA, conceived the notion of an annual publication showing off designers work, entitled simply *Designers in Britain*. This had a specific section on packaging design, sometimes showing off as many as thirty examples, including the work of DRU members as Gray, Collins and Norbert Dutton, but modestly not his own.

Dutton was similarly active in proselytising the contribution a designer could make to the economy. He was already concerning himself with packaging design prior to the war when he appears to have been operating on a freelance basis from a studio in Fleet Street. The 1936, *Marketing and Packaging Omnibus*, described him as 'The Metal Box Ltd. designer' for an article he wrote on 'The Mechanics of Package Design', extolling the virtue of the artist working to a brief –

'Many artists can create a striking design when given a free hand and no restrictions; only an outstanding designer can build around these restrictions the very basis of his design, producing finally a pack which satisfies at the same time both aesthetic and practical needs'.

Kenneth Lamble, Willy de Majo and Milner Grey, Gilbey corporate identy programme, 1959

Norbert Dutton and Milner Gray packaging for Hornimans Tea, 1940s

Norbert Dutton cosmetic packs for Cullingford, 1940s

Cecil Keeling designs for John Gaplin Ltd, 1950/51

In the article Dutton displays a real passion for his subject, the reader catching his sensitivity when he writes of the materials available to a package designer –

'Every material has its own characteristic possibilities, which should be exploited to the fullest extent'

not for Dutton 'bakelite looking like walnut' or 'tin printed to imitate wood'.

In 1938 Dutton contributed to the setting up of a design group – The Design Unit Limited – a news report of which in *Art & Industry* describing him then as a packaging expert. This group had echoes of Gray's Industrial Design Partnership and foretold the establishment of multi-specialist design teams after the war, as the Design Research Unit. Dutton is reported in the news item as considering many design commission, as only to be well carried out if undertaken by teams of designers. Presumably the onset of the war brought the Unit to an end.

Dutton's path seems to have crossed Gray's when they were working for the Ministry of Information during the war; and by the end of the war, Dutton had been welcomed into DRU as an associate. Dutton, as has been noted, had already a reputation as a package designer by the late 30s, not least for his iconic revision of Cadbury's labelling of its chocolate bars. Once with DRU his work was continuously referred to in the design press, his ingenious logo for Plessey being particularly lauded. He, himself, had many articles in design publications including *Design*, *The Architectural Review* and *Graphis*. When *Art & Industry* commissioned Dutton to review the inspiring design output of London Transport (he had done some textile designing for LT before the war), he was described as 'one of the best and most understanding of our younger generation of practical visionaries'.

By the 1950s, when DRU was getting in to its stride, Gray, himself, was in his 50s and considerably older than many of the young designers joining the Unit, Misha Black, for example, who had been a co-founder, being some ten years younger. Although when it came to packaging design, all had benefited from Gray's philosophy and methodology, some acting as his apostles, others began to find his meticulous supervision constraining and had to fly the nest to develop their own ideas.

The contribution of DRU to the development of packaging design after the war cannot be underestimated. With Gray's pioneering, it helped to make packaging a major element in the marketing of products. It raised the status of the humble packaging designer to that of change agent, albeit simultaneously demanding of the designer a pro-active multi-disciplined approach to a brief – if designers wanted professional status they had to earn it, was the message coming from the Unit.

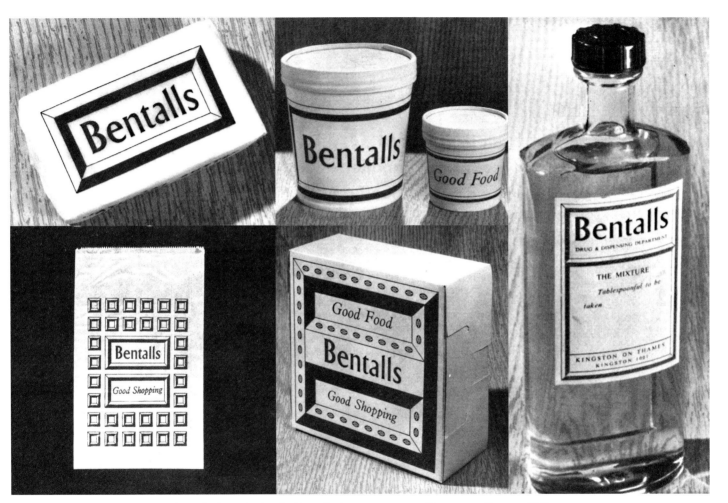

Peter Ray's packaging for Bentalls department store, Kingston on Thames, 1959

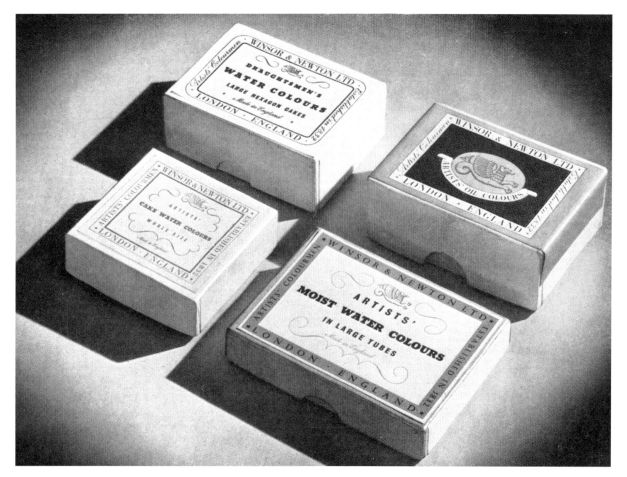

Jesse Collins for Windsor & Newton Ltd, 1940s

Jesse Collins for Martins Ltd, 1940s

Advertising and the Artist

ADVERTISING AGENCY PACKAGE DESIGNERS

'everything that needs to be told can be said to the trade and to the public in a manner that will not only be immediately recognizable, but will also evoke pleasant associations, thus achieving an ever increasing cumulative.' Ashley Havinden, Crawford Advertising

Packaging design was only occasionally offered as a service by advertising agencies, and, almost invariably, as one element of an advertising/publicity/ corporate identity campaign. There is rarely a mention of the word 'packaging' in the *Advertiser's Annuals,* even those for the 1950s when so much interesting packaging design was going on. A rare example of when the word appeared was for a London Press Exchange advertisement listing its studio's skills –

> *'turns rough scribbles for print, packaging and display materials into beautiful finished reality.'*

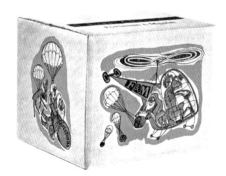

Fortnum and Mason Christmas, 1959

And that's about it! The artists employed by advertising agencies could be generally described as providing surface graphics rather than becoming fully involved in designing the packaging itself. And what contribution an agency artist made would depend, to some extent, on their personality and artistic inclinations, as well as on their status within the agency. Ashley Havinden, at Crawfords, was particularly interested in typography (referring to corporate identity as 'company handwriting'), and was sole art director; whereas Ruth Gill, also with a penchant for typography, at Colman, Prentis & Varley (CPV), was one of a number of art directors, each with their own team, handling their own clients. Gill, with a considerably wider agency experience than Havinden, would sometimes be working as much as an account executive as an artist, whilst Ashley, as he came to be known, had

Opposite: *Advertising and the Artist* by Ashley Havinden,1956

his wife Margaret, along with Crawford, handling the business side, leaving him relatively free to design.

Ruth Gill is particularly remembered for her work with Fortnum & Mason, carrying out some of the commissions herself, but often using the freelance artist Edward Bawden. Gill had actually been taught packaging design by Milner Gray when she was a student at Chelsea Art College, as well as being taught 'to see in the round' by Henry Moore. And when, on leaving college, she set up as a freelance with a friend, it was packaging design she offered, and it is possible her work for Jackson's of Piccadilly may well have come from that time.

Gill went on to join a small advertising agency, John Tait, where she worked for some ten years, eventually becoming its Art Director. There are examples of her packaging design at Tait's; one, a blue quilted Innoxa powder box, became something of a news item. Her work with Fortnum & Mason stemmed from when she joined CPV. She was to involve not only Bawden, but younger members of her team, including Margaret Edwards. Between 1955 and 1960 CPV worked on a variety of assignments for the store, Gill producing its 'F' & 'M' trademark that was to appear on practically everything to do with Fortnum's, including its packaging. Ben Duncan, a copywriter contemporary of Gill, wrote of her use of lettering –

'She treated letters of the alphabet as design elements, turning them sideways and upside down or mere smear brushworks…'

Wrapping paper designed by Kennedy North for
Fortnum & Mason, 1925

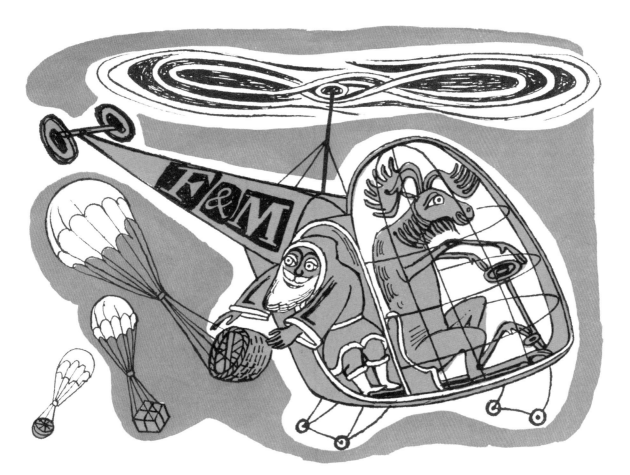

Edward Bawden illustration, Christmas 1959, for Ruth Gill,

Colman Prentis & Varley

Ruth Gill trademark for Fortnum & Mason, 1950s

Ruth Gill/ Mather & Crowther for Fisons Horticulture Ltd, 1960s

Ruth Gill/CPV designs for Ashe Laboratories, 'Headspin', 1950s

Ashley Havinden at WS Crawford Advertising, perfume packaging for Liberty, 1951

Frozen foods, stockings in see-through packs, gift boxes and wrapping paper packaging, designed by Ashley Havinden, 1960s

Examples given here are of her packaging for an all-purpose wrapping paper for the store's renowned tins of coffee and tea. Bawden mainly worked on catalogues, leaflets and the like, but there are odd examples of work he did on packaging, especially for christmas gifts.

Gill, herself, was involved in packaging design for a number of other companies, besides Fortnum's, including *Headspin* hair lotion and Bandbox shampoo for Ashe Laboratories, and for a range of products for French of London, the society hairdresser of the time, working for French with the young Margaret Edwards. Largely work was accredited to Gill, but occasionally Edwards got lone mention. When French's perfume and other products were illustrated in *Designers in Britain* there is a suggestion that the two were actually involved in the design of the shape of the packaging as well as its surface design.

Gill eventually left CPV for Mather & Crowther from where she did packaging designs for Fison's crop products.

Mary Gower, in her appreciation of the work of Gill as 'a creative mind in advertising', tells of critics who saw her work as so strong 'you'd never guess it was done by a woman'. This strength is clearly shown in her designs for packaging Fison's various bottles, cartons and sprays, her typography dominating the products, along with some use of photography to illustrate the plants likely to benefit from the use of the contents.

Ashley's perhaps best remembered packaging designs were those for a much publicized 'make-over' for Liberty's department store. In 1922 Ashley had been taken on by Crawford, as a raw untrained recruit, to help with the layout of advertisements. He was gradually to morph from ugly ducking to swan – to become one of the most suave, sophisticated graphic designers of his time. It was for Liberty's department store that he most successfully demonstrated his skill at 'company handwriting' –

'everything that needs to be told can be said to the trade and to the public in a manner that will not only be immediately recognizable, but will also evoke pleasant associations, thus achieving an ever increasing cumulative.'

Liberty's was embedded in the past, its building mock-Tudor, its floors strewn with 'arts and crafts'. Ashley was to bring modernism to the store. He began to experiment with the capital of its name – 'L' – which finally emerged from the drawing board larger than life, either in spots or stars, alongside it, smaller, but in bold type, the whole word – Liberty. This logo was to appear on all Liberty's packaging whether on bags and boxes for customers carrying purchases away, or on the wrapping of the articles themselves, as for scent bottles and see-through scarf packs.

Ashley's designs for Richard's shops packaging were equally striking, the words 'Richard's' and 'shops' made to look like labels attached to the wrapping, with a simple but strong background of loops. Ashley was to do similar work for other companies, including Pretty Polly stockings, but it was his work for Liberty's packaging that was to become iconic and to continue to be used by Liberty's for decades.

QUAKER
Wheat Munchies
ANTED!
CHILDREN
Send to Quaker Oats Limited, Southall, Middlesex, a photograph of your son or daughter. If our Advisory Panel think the child would make an attractive subject for the front of Quaker Wheat Munchies and Quaker Corn Flakes packages, we will call at your home and arrange with you to take a studio portrait of your child. In return for your permission to take and use your child's photograph, we will pay you the usual photographic modelling fees which will be not less than £5, and we will also present you with a beautifully framed studio portrait of your boy or girl.
Our Advisory Panel consists of a studio photographer, a package designer and Humphrey Lestocq, star of Radio and Children's Television.
We are looking for 8 boys or girls by 31st May 1955. A further 8 boys or girls by 31st August 1955, and a final 8 children by 30th November 1955. Send in your child's photo today. Remember, 24 children are wanted!
SCREEN TESTS!
They will be offered, too, the thrill of a lifetime—a trip for all four children and their families round a film studio, during which they will meet a famous film star. Then, on the basis of the film tests, two of the four children will be elected Quaker Boy and Quaker Girl for 1955. So here is a real opportunity for your boy or girl.
Don't delay, send off a photo of your son or daughter today to
DEPT. F, QUAKER OATS LIMITED
SOUTHALL MIDDLESEX
Don't forget to write your name and address on the back with the name and address of your grocer. Enclose a stamped addressed envelope if you want us to return the photograph.
QUAKER
Wheat Munchies
QUAKER
Wheat Munchies

OWN STUDIO DESIGNERS

HENRION, DE MAJO AND SCHLEGER

A number of designers, working alone or in small studios, offered packaging design as a service amongst a range of other graphic work. One of the most innovative of these was William Maks de May, known in Britain as W.M. de Majo, or to his most intimate associates, Willy. de Majo was as much, if not more, interested in the design of the total package as in the design of its surface, and was to produce some ingenuous solutions to packaging challenges.

Born in Vienna, of Yugoslav nationality, de Majo came to London in 1939, not as a refugee, but, curiously, as the leader of a Yugoslav boy scout delegation to a conference in Scotland! Although becoming naturalised British, and serving with other Yugoslavs as part of the RAF during the war (for which he was awarded an MBE), his was to remain international.

de Majo had had his own studio in Belgrade from around 1935, and, along with posters, advertisements and exhibitions, was even then offering packaging as a service. After his war service, he set up his own studio in London where, by the 1950s, packaging design featured large. Some of his assignments were one offs, some were done as elements of corporate identity programmes. He soon had established himself as something of an authority on packaging and in an article in *Art & Industry* in 1951 wrote with confidence –

> *'In this age of atoms, superlatives and science, it is amazing how little progress has been made in the art of packaging.'*

In the *Graphis* publication of 1959, devoted entirely to packaging design across the world, de Majo's work was illustrated more than that of any other British designer – his commissions from some ten different companies. In his article in the same publication, entitled *The Design of the Gift Pack* de Majo encouraged other artists to follow his lead –

Opposite: Wheat Munchies by Quaker, FHK Henrion, 1955

'If only they would broaden their horizon a little and direct some of their enthusiasm and imagination to the field of experimental construction work the thin ranks of packaging experts would be reinforced by their talents and they would have the added satisfaction of developing new dimensions in their work, both figuratively and literally.'

de Majo appears to have been particularly attracted to the challenge of designing packaging for awkwardly shaped goods – a shell-shaped perfume bottle for Delavelle, a pair of salad servers for Liberty's, a fountain pen for Miles Martin. But, in this respect, he was perhaps at his most ingenious with his packaging for Brades & Nash Tyzack Industries, makers of tools. Whether he was tackling the packaging of a garden spade or shears, he successfully managed to provide packs that would stack and display well, that displayed their contents clearly, and yet were protective of the goods they wrapped. For Brades and other firms de Majo was especially strong when it came to combination packs – a bottle and glasses, lipstick and powder, ties and handkerchiefs.

Generally de Majo seems to have been given sole credit for his designs (even when he was working with Gray for Gilbey's), but not infrequently he is named with his wife Veronica, and, for the odd item, with FHK Henrion. Occasionally an assistant's or illustrator's name was added to his as with P. Harvey for Miles Martin Pens, K. Toyne for Gilbey's drinking glasses, and Toyne and Robin Jacques for Gilbey's christmas packs for drink bottles

– but de Majo's name was always first. His practice was registered as 'W.M de Majo and associates' and ran from 1946 until his death in 1993, but apart from Veronica his 'associates' went largely unnamed.

de Majo was always international in his outlook. Before establishing himself in London he had worked not only in Belgrade, but in Scandinavia and Central and Southern Europe, aided, no doubt, by his being fluent in some four languages. At one time he had an office in New York, and he was to found, along with Peter Kneebone, the International Council of Graphic Design Associates (ICOGRADA) and to become its first President. His contribution to internationalism was recognized in 1969, when SIAD awarded him its Design Medal for International Services to Design and the Profession.

When the name FHK Henrion comes up there is an immediate mental link to his pioneering essays in corporate identity design and to his pavilion work for the Festival of Britain. Yet an unpublished obituary by Michael Peters has –

'I had not realised until reviewing his packaging work, how even today (with all the sophisticated marketing and research techniques that are used to aid and abet packaging design) how advanced was Henrion's work. His skill as an architect of cardboard construction, his dynamic used of colour and illustration and his communication skills as art director have made his work some of the most influential and impressive over the last thirty years.'

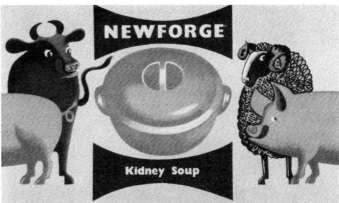

Soup tin labels designed by Henrion with de Majo, 1952

WM de Majo/K Joyne/Robin Jacques for Gilbey's, 1959

de Majo (labels designed by Milner Gray) for W. & A. Gilbey ltd, 1956/7

de Majo packaging for Liberty, 1959

FHK Henrion, born in Germany in 1914, had a career that could be said to be divided into three parts – first as a graphic designer of posters, advertisements and magazines; secondly as a designer of corporate identity schemes; and thirdly as an educator and international proselytiser of graphic design. With little formal design training he had come to London in 1936 to carry out a commission and had stayed on to work, during the war, for the Ministry of Information. On becoming naturalised in 1946, he set up his own design consultancy, Studio H, which morphed, as his reputation grew, into Henrion Design Associates, and, finally, into HDA International.

He could well have been introduced to packaging design when his friend, Landauer, helped him obtain temporary work with Milner Gray's Industrial Design Partnership; and it is thought that it was through Gray he obtained work for the Ministry of Information, for he was strictly an alien at the time.

Within his consultancy Henrion was to produce packaging graphics for a wide variety of products – beer, breakfast cereals, tinned foods, printing ink and toilet paper; and he would, additionally, provide logos for a number of companies to appear on their packaging. His wrap around labels for Newforge soup tins, designed with de Majo, caused a ripple in the design press in that when carefully placed side by side, on a display shelf, they made a frieze of poultry. This may have been fun to design but must have proved irritating to the hard-pressed shelf filler who had to see that the tins were in an appropriate sequence.

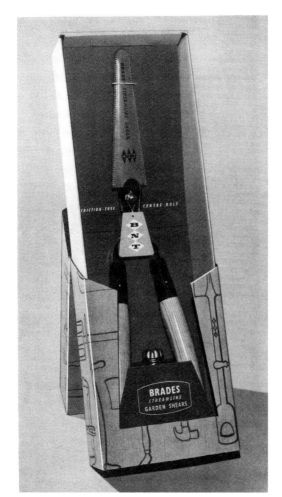

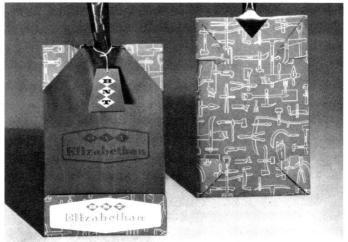

de Majo's tool packaging for Brades Nash Tyzack Industries, 1959

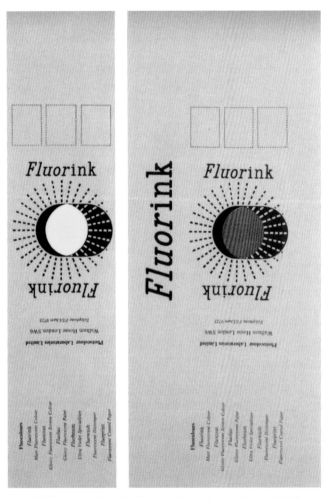

FHK Henrion labels for Photocolour Laboratories Ltd, 1952

But Henrion's approach to design generally, which would have affected his packaging design was hard-headed and practical. For him information put on packaging was pruned down to absolute essentials, and the design steered away from the glitzy or excessively decorative. He wrote –

'Self-expression of the designer is rarely required, though creative imagination is always needed channelled within the objective set conditions.'

As something of a polymath, interested in the social and economic aspects of design, as well as the scientific, technical and aesthetic, he did, as Peters suggested, produce some striking work, perhaps his best arising out of his large scale commissions for corporate identity design. He wrote of this change of focus –

'I have become accustomed to doing all sorts of things – stationery, emblems, layout and packaging. It occurred to me that it would be sensible to have fewer clients but to be in charge of all their design projects.'

And it is within his various 'all design' projects that Henrion produced some strong packaging designs – from his early work for Bowaters and Pest Control Ltd, in the late 1940s and early 1950s, through to his comprehensive consultancies for KLM, BEA, Tate & Lyle and Blue Circle Cement in the 60s. There could hardly have been a pantry in the country that did not contain a bag

Sugar packaging as part of the Tate & Lyle corporate identity scheme, Henrion Design Associates, 1960s

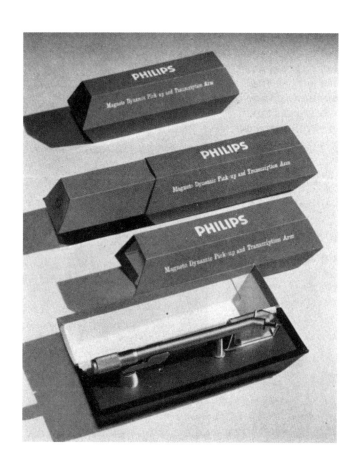

FHK Henrion design for pick-up arm for Philips, 1950s

FHK Henrion carrier for Olivetti typewriters, 1960s

Henrion Design Associates Corporate identity design for Blue Circle, the grouping together of
more than twenty allied companies, 1968

of Tate & Lyle sugar, the pack puritanically designed with just the manufacturer's name, the contents and the weight – just a very few words, in blue lettering standing out from a white background – but that sufficed for a user to immediately pick it out, whether on a supermarket shelf or in a larder.

Henrion's packaging designs seem to have been largely surface graphics but there is the odd example of where he has been involved in the actual construction of a package for which Peters had so admired his skills – a pick-up arm for Philips, for which an inner pack holding the arm fits into an outer sleeve, and a carrier for Olivetti typewriters.

In his later years Henrion became Head of Graphic Design at the then London College of Printing and was recognized for his outstanding contribution to design with an OBE in 1984.

Hans Schleger was yet another graphic designer working from his own studio of a few assistants, who did packaging design, usually within a corporate identity design programme. As with de Majo and Henrion, Schleger was a naturalised Britain, born and trained in Berlin but with a wealth of design experience behind him before arriving in London in 1933. He had not only operated in Germany (where he had been art director for the Crawford agency), but had had considerable success in America working for fashion houses. After WWII he worked for a time as a consultant to the advertising agency Mather & Crowther (1951-62), Hans Schleger & Associates not formerly established until 1954. He was to work on commissions from his studio in Chelsea for some forty years until his death in 1976.

Schleger's most extensive packaging designs were for Mac Fisheries, then a large scale firm concerned with most aspects of fishery, with a considerable number of retail high street shops. After a good deal of consultation with key personnel and the studio awash with actual fish for some time, Schleger made, in all, some seven hundred designs, including a logo (four fishes within a St. Andrews cross), along with a jolly little figure of a fish to lighten the message. His brief had included the caution 'impact without vulgarity', and that is what he achieved in his packaging. For Mac Fisheries frozen food range Schleger's colour coding made for easy selection, as noted earlier;

Evolution of the Mac Fisheries symbol, 1952

Hans Schleger for Mac Fisheries, colour coding system, 1956

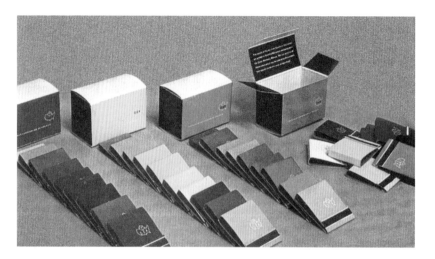

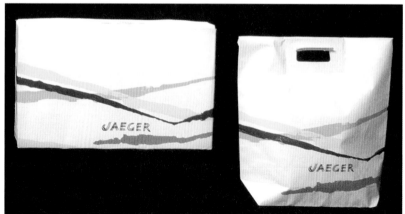

Colour harmonies match books for the Container Corporation of America,
1951 and designs for Jaeger carrier bags and boxes, 1958/60

Schleger's prototype bottle design for Grants whisky, 1955-6

Watermen's encapsulated pen for point of sale display, 1952

and his forming the word 'fresh' in handwriting stood out from the background of the packs – a device he used for a number of his designs as it echoed the fishmonger writing up the daily catch on his slate.

Schleger's designs for sugar packets for the British Sugar Corporation suggest that he leaned rather more towards artistry and self-expression in his work than did those of the Milner Gray school of packaging design, albeit he did emphasise the Britishness of the product with his colours – red, white and blue – making the packs distinct from those of its competitor Tate & Lyle. His designs for the packs were chosen for display in the Packaging Exhibition at the Design Centre in 1965. When writing about the commission Schleger's ego protrudes –

'I like to come to the problem without any luggage or pre-conceived notions, to discover the situation for myself and work on it simply, on my level of experience…'

Milner Gray was all about 'pre-conceived notions' derived from research, consultation and data analysis. An example of Schleger's ego getting the better of him was when he was given a commission, in 1955, to design a bottle and label for Grant's whisky with the brief that it must be distinctive, elegant, competitive and clearly show the quality and colour of the product. Well he both won and lost – he came up with the daring idea of a triangular bottle which he felt the hand could grasp more firmly than when more open around a cylindrical bottle – it would

certainly have been distinctive for there were no such shaped whisky bottles on the market at the time. He first sculpted the bottle out of clay and then out of plaster of Paris, carefully working out the weight of the contents by its displacement in a bucket of water. For this his courageous creativity won the day, inspite of the additional production expense involved. But when he wanted the graphics fired into the glass he had gone a step too far and Grants insisted on keeping its traditional label. Pat Schleger, in loyal defence of her husband, recorded how *The Director* magazine supported him –

'the design world criticises the retention of the old label, it should have been redesigned to tailor with the new shape.'

Incidental to his main graphic design for advertising and publicity Schleger also did display stands and packaging for Waterman's pens, match books for the Container Corporation of America, some packaging for Finmar (with his iconic logo of a bare tree), packs for Raven Knitwear and a variety of boxes and bags for Jaeger customers with simple yet strong overlapping coloured lines.

Sugar package design for British Sugar Corporation, 1961

Finmar Furniture, Coffee Master carrier box , 1959

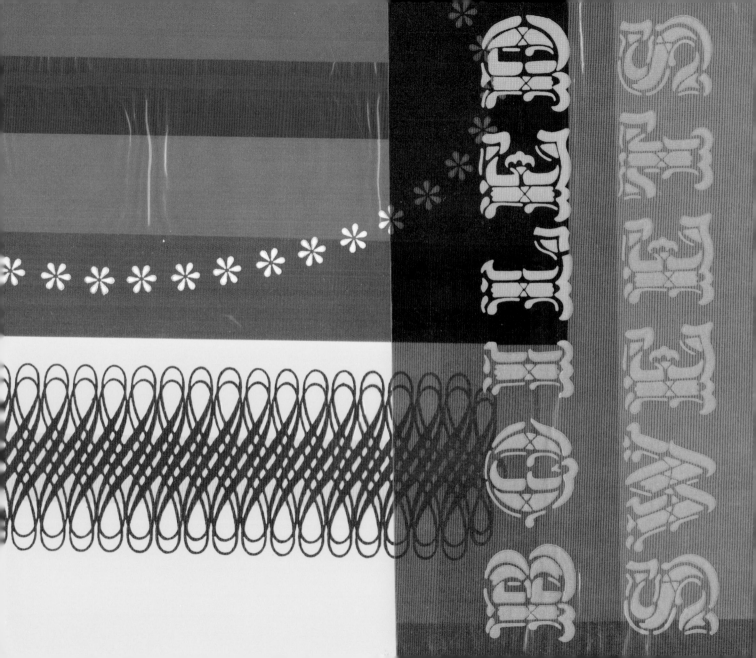

EPILOGUE

Some readers may consider this to have been an unjustified celebration of packaging and its designers. I can only hope that by now the reader can pick up any package and delight in its appropriateness, yet be critical of its excesses. I hope that the reader now can, more objectively and calmly, question in what ways packaging does its job and where it falls short – can you pick it out quickly on a supermarket shelf; does it tell you all you need to know, legibly; has it arrived home in perfect order; can it be stacked and stored easily, opened and shut, used and reused, and remain intact.

It is clear that much packaging is unnecessary and that some materials used are a threat to our environment. This needs serious consideration and action rather than mere promises and declarations from manufacturers, retailers and government. One can only hope a government comes along that has the clout and the will for this. Let us hope for well-designed economic packaging in the future – and an appropriate appreciation of the ingenuity and creativity of the packaging designer.

SAINSBURY'S
beans
in tomato sauce
SAINSBURY'S
beans
in tomato sauce
SAINSBURY'S
beans
in tomato sauce
SAINSBURY'S
beans
in tomato sauce
SAINSBURY'S
beans
in tomato sauce
SAINSBURY'S
beans
in tomato sauce

BIBLIOGRAPHY

1937 D.E.A. Charlton, *The Art of Packaging*, The Studio Ltd.

1938 *Omnibus of Marketing and Packaging*, Creative Journals

1947 Alec Davis, *Package & Print*, Faber & Faber

1951 Alec Davis, *Type in Advertising*, Raithby Lawrence

1955 Milner Gray, *Package Design*, The Studio Publications

1959 ed. Walter Herdeg, *Packaging*, Graphis

1962 ed. F.A.Paine, *Fundamentals of Packaging*, Blackie & Son

1969 John & Avril Blake, *The Practical Idealists* Lund Humphries

1986 Avril Blake, *Milner Gray*, The Design Council

1991 Howard Milton, *Packaging Design*, The Design Council

1992 Jerry Jankowski, *Shelf Life*, Chronicle Books

1995 Robert Fitzgerald, *Rowntree & the Marketing Revolution*, Cambridge Univeristy Press

1996 ed. Mona Doyle, *Packaging Strategy*, Technomic

1998 Jerry Jankowski, *Shelf Space*, Chronicle Books

2008 John Bradley, *Cadbury's Purple Reign*, Wiley

2009 Van Wilson, *The Story of Terry's*, York Oral History Soc

2010 Michelle Cotton, *Design Research Unit 1942-72*, Koenig Books

2011 Ruth Artmonsky, *FHK Henrion*, Design A.C.C. Art Books

2011 Jonny Trunk, *Own Label*, Fuel

2012 Paul Chrystal, *Cadbury & Fry*, Amberley

2013 Timothy Dickson, *Leonard Beaumont*, Derwent-Wye

2013 John Bradley, *Fry's Chocolate Dream*, Yknot Publishing

2014 Ruth Artmonsky, *Moving the Hearts and Minds of Men, Bill Crawford Ad Man*, Artmonsky Arts

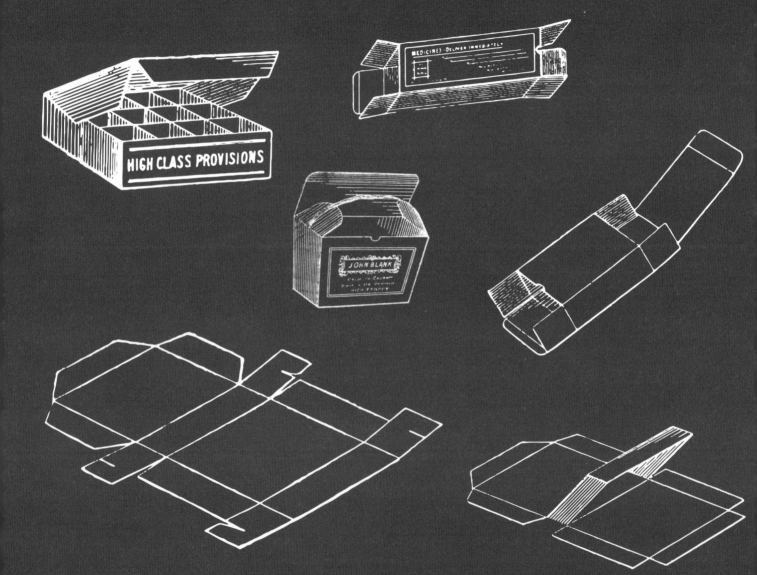

OTHER BOOKS BY RUTH ARTMONSKY

Jack Beddington, a footnote man, 2006
The School Prints, 2006
Art for Everyone, 2007
A Snapper up of Unconsidered Trifles, 2008
Bringers of Good Tidings, 2009
Shipboard Style, 2010
'Do you want it good or do you want it Tuesday?', 2011
Designing Women, 2012
The Pleasures of Printing, 2013
Showing Off, 2013
Exhibiting Ourselves, 2014
Moving the Hearts and Minds of Men, 2014
Unashamed Artists, 2014
Art for the Ear, 2015
Here's to Your Health, (with Stella Harpley), 2015

Tom Purvis: Art for the Sake of Money, 2015
The Best Advertising Course in Town, 2015
Powering the Home, 2016
From Palaces to Pre-Fabs, 2017
The Golden Age of British Advertising, 2018

P&O, a history, Shire Publications, 2012
P&O, across the oceans, across the years,
Antique Collectors' Club, 2012

The Design series with Brian Webb published by
Antique Collector's Club –
Design, Lewitt-Him, 2008
Design, FHK Henrion, 2011
Design, Enid Marx, 2013